CONTENTS

THE HISTORY OF SCALES & MODES

The word scale is derived from the Latin and Italian word "scala" meaning ladder, which is precisely what a scale is - a sequential order of adjoining notes either ascending or descending an octave in stepwise order. Scales form the foundation of music of various people, places and periods.

It is believed that the earliest form of scales originated with the ancient Greeks and were labeled according to their most important tribes; the Dorian, Phrygian, Lydian and Mixolydian. These scales consisted of eight notes counting the octave. The Dorian scale descended from E, the Phrygian scale descended from D, the Lydian scale descended from C and the Mixolydian scale descended from B.

The early Christian church adopted these scales but they reversed the order so that the scales ascended rather than descended and the notes from which they started were altered. The Greek Dorian scale became the Dorian mode and ascended from D to D, the Phrygian mode ascended from E to E, the Lydian mode ascended from F to F and the Mixolydian mode ascended from G to G. The word mode was used instead of scale and is derived from the Latin word "modus" meaning manner or method.

The Greek Lydian scale which descended from C became the Ionian mode and ascended from C, the Greek Mixolydian scale which descended from B became the Locrian mode and ascended from B and the scale that started on A became the the Aeolian mode.

<u>The Ionian mode</u> begins on the first degree of the major scale and is the same as the major scale. <u>The Dorian mode</u> begins on the second degree of the major scale and is a natural minor scale with a raised (major) sixth. <u>The Phrygian mode</u> begins on the third degree of the major scale and is a natural minor scale with a lowered (minor) second. <u>The Lydian mode</u> begins on the fourth degree of the major scale and is the same as a major scale with a raised (major) fourth. <u>The Mixolydian mode</u> begins on the fifth degree of the major scale and is a major scale with a lowered (minor) seventh. <u>The Aeolian mode</u> begins on the sixth degree of the major scale and is the same as a natural minor scale. <u>The Locrian mode</u> begins on the seventh degree of the major scale and is a natural minor scale with the lowered (minor) second and fifth. This scale has a diminished sound.

Mel Bay's

Encyclopedia of Scales & Modes for Electric Bass

By
Dana Roth

1 2 3 4 5 6 7 8 9 0

INTRODUCTION

When I became interested in the bass guitar,
my dream was to become a top session player.

I bought all the bass books
I could find and sought private instruction.

Over the years, I studied and played.

The books I used were informative,
however, I was unable to find one that contained
all the information I wanted to use as a reference.

With help from many sources,
I began to compile my own notes
in a more concise format.

These notes became my book,
ENCYCLOPEDIA OF SCALES & MODES FOR ELECTRIC BASS

Preface

The proficient bass player has a thorough knowledge of scales and modes. Learning them will expand an awareness and ability to improvise in any situation. This method of study enables the bassist to easily become familiar with the various forms of scales and modes. There are extensive fingerboard diagrams to the 24th fret, formulas, charts and applications utilizing each scale or mode. Sight reading is not necessary to understand this material as bass tablature is provided, along with standard musical notation.

About the Author

Dana Roth was born in Encino, California, in 1966. Her fascination with the bass guitar began at an early age. After performing in a succession of original rock groups and studying with bass instructors, she became interested in the theory of music and began writing bass books. Dana continues to be active in her bass playing and is in the process of designing a line of bass guitars. She resides in Newport Beach, California.

MODES

C MAJOR SCALE (2 OCTAVES)

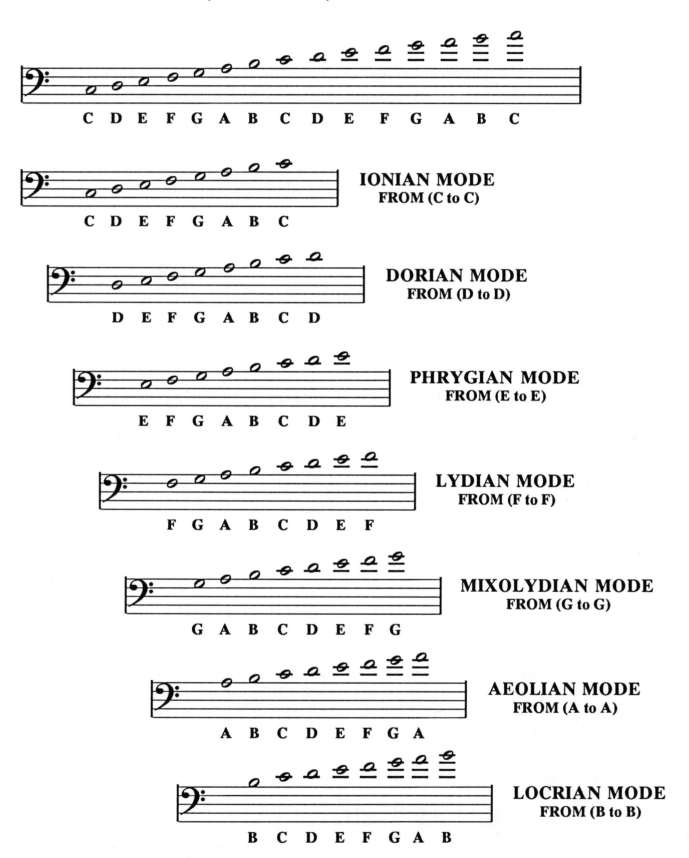

C D E F G A B C D E F G A B C

IONIAN MODE
FROM (C to C)

C D E F G A B C

DORIAN MODE
FROM (D to D)

D E F G A B C D

PHRYGIAN MODE
FROM (E to E)

E F G A B C D E

LYDIAN MODE
FROM (F to F)

F G A B C D E F

MIXOLYDIAN MODE
FROM (G to G)

G A B C D E F G

AEOLIAN MODE
FROM (A to A)

A B C D E F G A

LOCRIAN MODE
FROM (B to B)

B C D E F G A B

5

MAJOR SCALE VS. MINOR SCALES

The *Major Scale* is a series of eight notes (including the octave) and there is a semi-tone between the 3rd and 4th and the 7th and 8th degrees.

C Major Scale

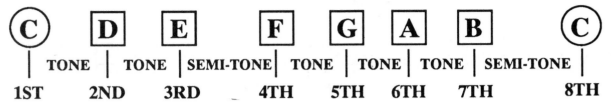

The *Natural Minor Scale* is a series of eight notes (including the octave) with a semi-tone between the 2nd and 3rd and the 5th and 6th degrees.

C Natural Minor Scale

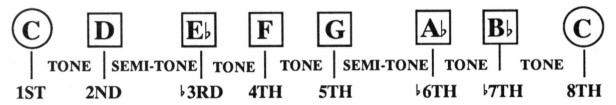

The *Harmonic Minor Scale* is like the natural minor scale with the 7th degree raised a semi-tone resulting in 3 semi-tones between the 6th and 7th degrees. This scale is a compromise between the ascending and descending melodic varieties. It is considered to be the basis of harmony in the minor keys.

C Harmonic Minor Scale

The *Melodic Minor Scale* either ascends or descends the octave; the *ascending* form of the melodic minor is like the natural minor scale with the 6th and 7th degrees raised a semi-tone. The *descending* form of the Melodic Minor Scale is the same as the Mixolydian mode and the descending form of the natural minor scale.

C Melodic Minor Scale (Ascending)

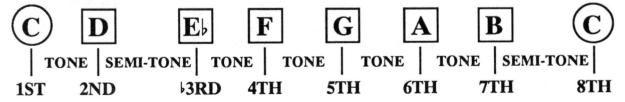

THE PENTATONIC SCALES

The *Pentatonic Scales* orinignated in the Far East and are one of the oldest scales of all. The word pentatonic is derived from the Greek word "penta" meaning five. These scales have five notes in which the octave is reached on the sixth note and some of the notes are more than a whole-tone apart. The *Major Pentatonic Scale* skips the 4th and 7th degrees of the major scale. The *Minor Pentatonic Scale* differs from the natural minor scale; the 2nd and 6th degrees are left out.

C MAJOR PENTATONIC

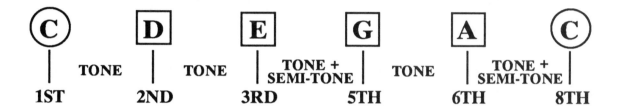

C MINOR PENTATONIC

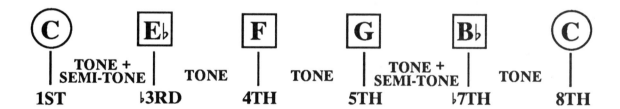

BLUES SCALE

The *Blues Scale* is similar to the major scale but the 3rd, 5th, and 7th degrees are lowered a semi-tone. The 6th degree is lowered two semi-tones.

C BLUES SCALE

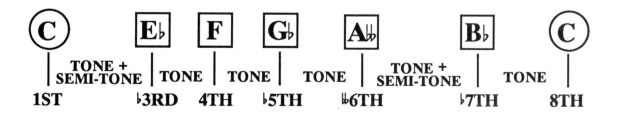

SYNTHETIC SCALES

Melody and harmony are dominated by the major scale, however many other scales can be created by selecting a different step pattern from the twelve semi-tone intervals of the chromatic scale and are called *Synthetic Scales.*

The *Chromatic Scale* consists of twelve degrees and either ascends or descends the octave by semi-tones.

THE CHROMATIC SCALE
FORMULA
Root +1/2+1/2+1/2+1/2+1/2+1/2+1/2+1/2+1/2+1/2+1/2 /octave
EXAMPLE-KEY OF C

C	C#	D	D#	E	F	F#	G	G#	A	A#	B	C

The most commonly used synthetic scales are the *Whole-tone Scale, Diminished Scale* and the *Pentatonic Scales.* These scales are often used in modern music.

The *Whole-Tone Scale* separates the octave into six whole-tone intervals without any semi-tones. The sound of the whole-tone scale is the same no matter which note it starts from and only two whole-tone scales are needed to cover all twelve keys; the C whole-tone scale and the C# or D♭ whole-tone scales.

THE WHOLE-TONE SCALE
FORMULA
Root +1+1+1+1+1 /octave
EXAMPLE-KEY OF C

C	D	E	F#	G#	A#	C

The *Diminished Scale* separates the octave into eight intervals of whole-tones and semi-tones. This scale consists of nine notes including the octave. Every diminished scale has four possible key centers in its scale; the 1st, 3rd, 5th, and 7th degrees. Only three diminished scales are needed to cover all twelve keys; the C diminished scale, C# or D♭ diminished scale and the D diminished scale.

THE DIMINISHED SCALE
FORMULA
Root +1+1/2+1+1/2+1+1/2+1 /octave
EXAMPLE-KEY OF C

C	D	E♭	F	G♭	G#	A	B	C

These four *synthetic scales* are considered to be "dissonent" and they present other melodic variations.

The *Neapolitan Scale* is different from the major scale; the 2nd and 3rd degrees are lowered a semi-tone.

THE NEAPOLITAN SCALE
FORMULA
Root +1/2+1+1+1+1+1 /octave
EXAMPLE-KEY OF C

C	D♭	E♭	F	G	A	B	C

The *Neapolitan Minor Scale* is different from the major scale; the 2nd, 3rd, and 6th degree are lowered a semi-tone.

THE NEAPOLITAN MINOR SCALE
FORMULA
Root +1/2+1+1+1+1/2+1 1/2 /octave
EXAMPLE-KEY OF C

C	D♭	E♭	F	G	A♭	B	C

The *Hungarian Minor Scale* is different from the major scale; the 3rd and 6th degrees are lowered a semi-tone and the 4th degree is raised a semi-tone.

THE HUNGARIAN MINOR SCALE
FORMULA
Root +1+1/2+1 1/2+1/2+1/2+1 1/2 /octave
EXAMPLE-KEY OF C

C	D	E♭	F♯	G	A♭	B	C

The *Enigmatic Scale* is different from the major scale; the 2nd degree is lowered a semi-tone and the 4th, 5th and 6th degrees are raised a semi-tone.

THE ENIGMATIC SCALE
FORMULA
Root +1/2+1 1/2+1+1+1+1/2 /octave
EXAMPLE-KEY OF C

C	D♭	E	F♯	G♯	A♯	B	C

FORMULAS

MAJOR SCALE - This scale can be used on any progression in the same key.
Formula: Root + 1 + 1 + 1/2 + 1 + 1 + 1 + octave

NATURAL MINOR SCALE - This scale can be played over minor chords.
Formula: Root + 1 + 1/2 + 1 + 1 + 1/2 + 1 + octave

MAJOR PENTATONIC - This scale is related to the major scale, you can use it whenever you play the major scale.
Formula: Root + 1 + 1 + 1 1/2 + 1 + octave

MINOR PENTATONIC - This scale can be used with minor chords.
Formula: Root + 1 1/2 + 1 + 1 + 1 1/2 + octave

BLUES SCALE - This scale can be used on minor and dominant 7th chords.
Formula: Root + 1 1/2 + 1 + 1/2 + 1/2 + 1 1/2 + octave

MIXOLYDIAN MODE - This mode can be used with dominant 7th chords, C7, D7, G7, etc.
Formula: Root + 1 + 1 + 1/2 + 1 + 1 + 1/2 + octave

DORIAN MODE - This mode can be played over minor chords. It is often used in rock 'n' roll and jazz.
Formula: Root + 1 + 1/2 + 1 + 1 + 1 + 1/2 + octave

LYDIAN MODE - This mode can be used with major 7th chords.
Formula: Root + 1 + 1 + 1 + 1/2 + 1 + 1 + octave

PHRYGIAN MODE - This mode can be played over minor chords.
Formula: Root + 1/2 + 1 + 1 + 1 + 1/2 + 1 + octave

LOCRIAN MODE - This mode is similar to the natural minor. It can be used on minor chords and also diminished chords.
Formula: Root + 1/2 + 1 + 1 + 1/2 + 1 + 1 + octave

HARMONIC MINOR - It is the same as the natural minor form, but with a raised seventh degree.
Formula: Root + 1 + 1/2 + 1 + 1 + 1/2 + 1 1/2 + octave

MELODIC MINOR *(Ascending)* - It is the same as the natural minor form, but with raised sixth and raised seventh degrees.
Formula: Root + 1 + 1/2 + 1 + 1 + 1 + 1 + octave

MELODIC MINOR *(Descending)* - It is the same as the natural minor scale or the aeolian mode.
Formula: Root + 1 + 1/2 + 1 + 1 + 1/2 + 1 + octave

AEOLIAN MODE - It is the same as the natural minor form. It can be played over minor chords.
Formula: Root + 1 + 1/2 + 1 + 1 + 1/2 + 1 + octave

IONIAN MODE - It is the same as the major scale form. It can be used on any progression in the same key.
Formula: Root + 1 + 1 + 1/2 + 1 + 1 + 1 + octave

KEY SIGNATURES

C MAJOR / A MINOR
No Sharps Or Flats

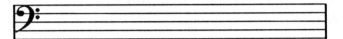

G MAJOR / E MINOR
1 Sharp F♯

D MAJOR / B MINOR
2 Sharps F♯ - C♯

A MAJOR / F♯ MINOR
3 Sharps F♯ - C♯ - G♯

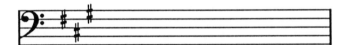

E MAJOR / C♯ MINOR
4 Sharps F♯ - C♯ - G♯ - D♯

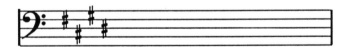

B MAJOR / G♯ MINOR
5 Sharps F♯ - C♯ - G♯ - D♯ - A♯

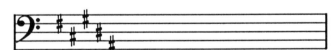

F♯ MAJOR / D♯ MINOR
6 Sharps F♯ - C♯ - G♯ - D♯ - A♯ - E♯

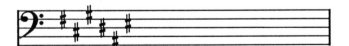

F MAJOR / D MINOR
1 Flat B♭

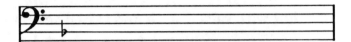

B♭ MAJOR / G MINOR
2 Flats B♭ - E♭

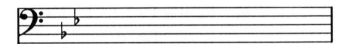

E♭ MAJOR / C MINOR
3 Flats B♭ - E♭ - A♭

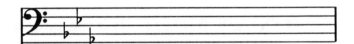

A♭ MAJOR / F MINOR
4 Flats B♭ - E♭ - A♭ - D♭

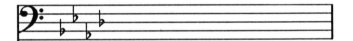

D♭ MAJOR / B♭ MINOR
5 Flats B♭ - E♭ - A♭ - D♭ - G♭

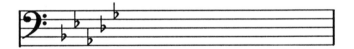

G♭ MAJOR / E♭ MINOR
6 Flats B♭ - E♭ - A♭ - D♭ - G♭ - C♭

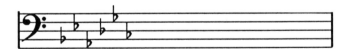

C♭ MAJOR / A♭ MINOR
7 Flats B♭ - E♭ - A♭ - D♭ - G♭ - C♭ - F♭

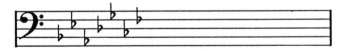

C♯ MAJOR / A♯ MINOR
7 Sharps F♯ - C♯ - G♯ - D♯ - A♯ - E♯ - B♯

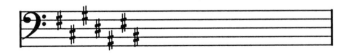

THE CIRCLE OF FIFTHS

The *Circle of Fifths* is a visual description of a series of fifths tuned in equal temperament, so that the twelfth note in the series has the same letter name as the first note. It is an arrangement of the twelve keys so that the amount of sharps in the key signature increases clockwise. The amount of flats in the key signature increases counterclockwise. All the keys and their enharmonic relationships are shown on the Circle of Fifths.

Enharmonic keys are two keys which have the same sound but have different key signatures. There are three enharmonic major keys; C♯ / D♭ - F♯ / G♭ - B/ C♭ and three enharmonic minor keys; B♭/ A♯ - E♭/ D♯ - A♭ / G♯ .

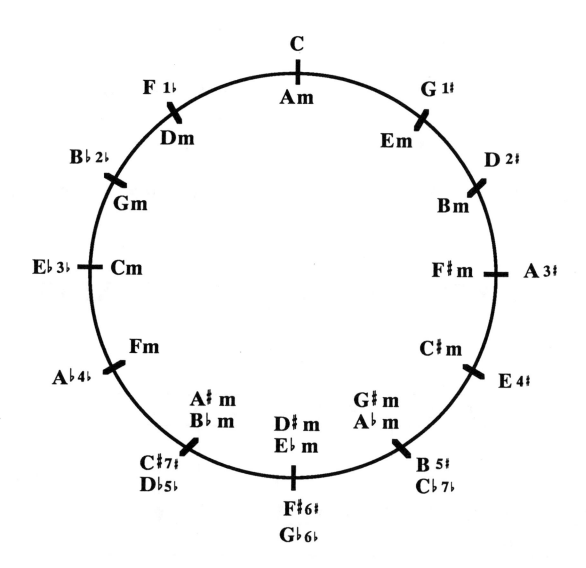

RELATIVE MAJOR & MINOR KEYS
HAVE IDENTICAL KEY SIGNATURES

CHROMATIC SIGNS   (ACCIDENTALS)

The Sharp Sign ♯ Raises the pitch of the note one semi-tone.

C♯ = D♭   D♯ = E♭   E♯ = F   F♯ = G♭   G♯ = A♭   A♯ = B♭   B♯ = C

The Double Sharp Sign ✕ Raises the pitch of the note a whole-tone or two semi-tones.

C✕ = D   D✕ = E   E✕ = F♯   F✕ = G   G✕ = A   A✕ = B   B✕ = C♯

The Flat Sign ♭ Lowers the pitch of the note one semi-tone.

C♭ = B   D♭ = C♯   E♭ = D♯   F♭ = E   G♭ = F♯   A♭ = G♯   B♭ = A♯

The Double Flat Sign ♭♭ Lowers the pitch of the note a whole-tone or two semi-tones.

C♭♭ = B♭   D♭♭ = C   E♭♭ = D   F♭♭ = E♭   G♭♭ = F   A♭♭ = G   B♭♭ = A

The Natural Sign ♮ Alters the pitch of the note to its original form.

C♮ = C   D♮ = D   E♮ = E   F♮ = F   G♮ = G   A♮ = A   B♮ = B

MAJOR KEYS & RELATIVE MINOR KEYS

Major Keys

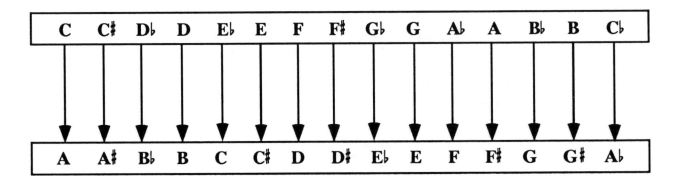

Relative Minor Keys

14

MAJOR SCALE CHART

Root	2nd	3rd	4th	5th	6th	7th	Octave
C	D	E	F	G	A	B	C
C♯	D♯	E♯	F♯	G♯	A♯	B♯	C♯
D♭	E♭	F	G♭	A♭	B♭	C	D♭
D	E	F♯	G	A	B	C♯	D
D♯	E♯	F×	G♯	A♯	B♯	C×	D♯
E♭	F	G	A♭	B♭	C	D	E♭
E	F♯	G♯	A	B	C♯	D♯	E
F	G	A	B♭	C	D	E	F
F♯	G♯	A♯	B	C♯	D♯	E♯	F♯
G♭	A♭	B♭	C♭	D♭	E♭	F	G♭
G	A	B	C	D	E	F♯	G
G♯	A♯	B♯	C♯	D♯	E♯	F×	G♯
A♭	B♭	C	D♭	E♭	F	G	A♭
A	B	C♯	D	E	F♯	G♯	A
A♯	B♯	C♯	D♯	E♯	F×	G♯	A♯
B♭	C	D	E♭	F	G	A	B♭
B	C♯	D♯	E	F♯	G♯	A♯	B

15

FRETBOARD CHART

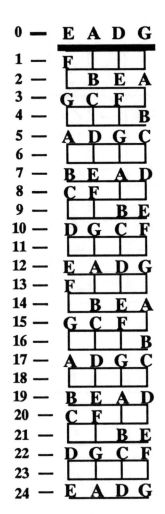

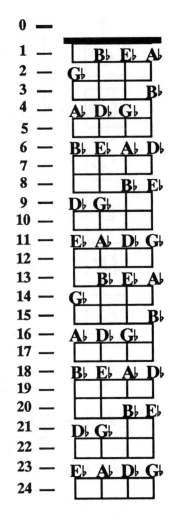

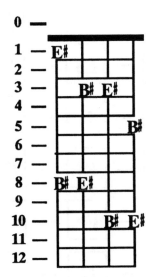

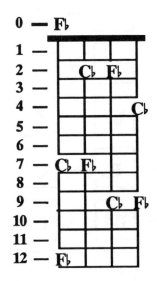

STANDARD BASS NOTATION

The *Staff* is a series of lines and spaces on which music is written. There are five parallel horizontal lines and four spaces. The lines are numbered from the bottom being 1, to the top being 5. The spaces are also numbered from the bottom, 1 to 4.

Example Of The Staff:

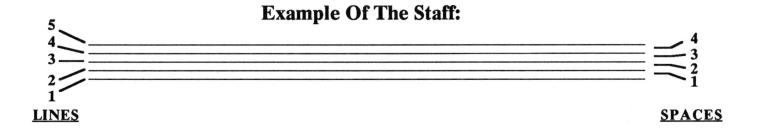

LINES   **SPACES**

The Bass Clef $\mathcal{9}$: This symbol is also known as the F Clef and it is placed at the begining of the staff to indicate pitch.

A staff with a Bass Clef symbol is called a Bass Staff.

Example:

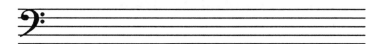

Symbols called "notes" are placed in the staff either on the lines or in the spaces. Their location on the staff indicates their pitch.

Ledger Lines are short lines that go above or below the staff to indicate pitches that exceed the limits of the five-line staff.

PRACTICE TIPS

Subjects To Practice

* **Play The Notes On The Neck To Warm Up.**

* **Octaves**

* **Reading**

* **Play The Scales And Modes Ascending And Then In Descending Order.**

   Example: C Major

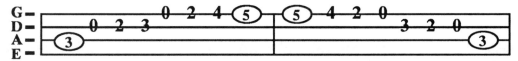

* **Take A Break**

* **Practice The Scales And Modes In All Twelve Keys.**

* **Try Playing The Scales And Modes In Open Position, Then Finish In 3rd Position Or Positions Of Your Choice.**

   Example: C Major

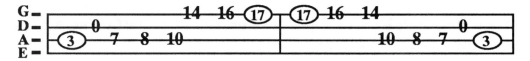

* **Try Making Up Your Own Riffs.**

* **Take A Break**

* **Most Important - <u>Have Fun With It</u> !**

BASS TABLATURE

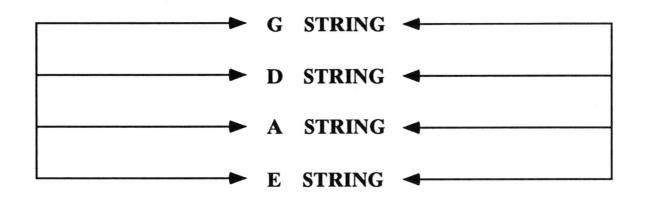

Example: **E Major**

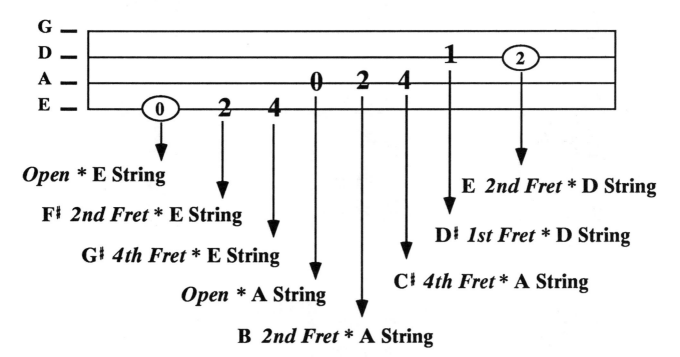

EXAMPLES OF SCALES AND MODES
IN ANY KEY □ = KEY NOTE

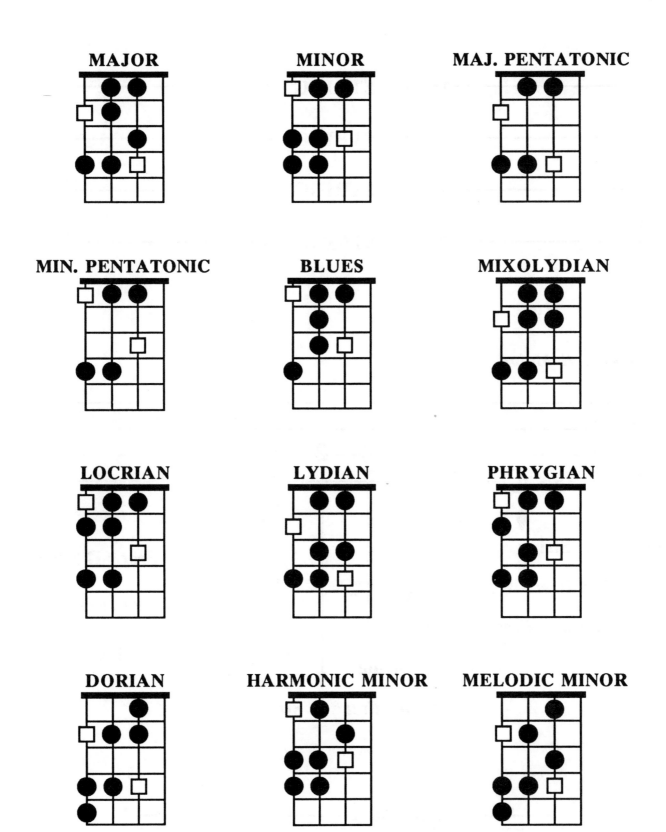

C MAJOR SCALE

FORMULA - (C) Root (D) 2nd (E) 3rd (F) 4th (G) 5th (A) 6th (B) 7th

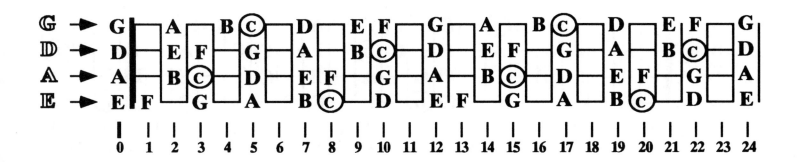

Positions

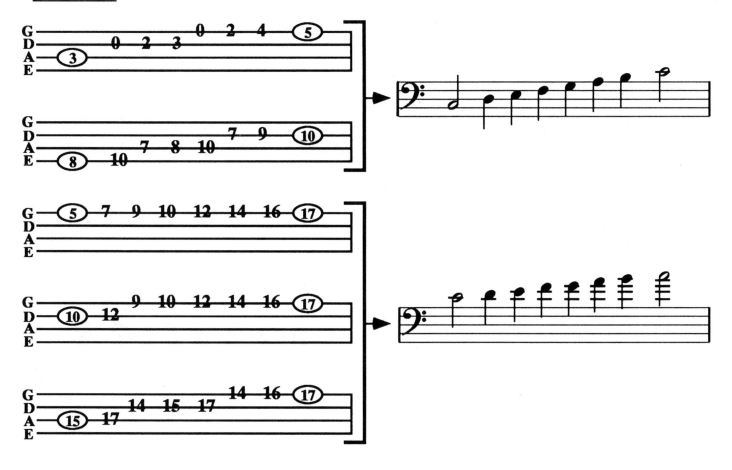

Riff

D MAJOR SCALE

FORMULA - (D) Root (E) 2nd (F♯) 3rd (G) 4th (A) 5th (B) 6th (C♯) 7th

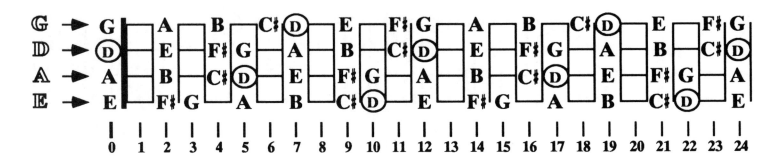

Positions

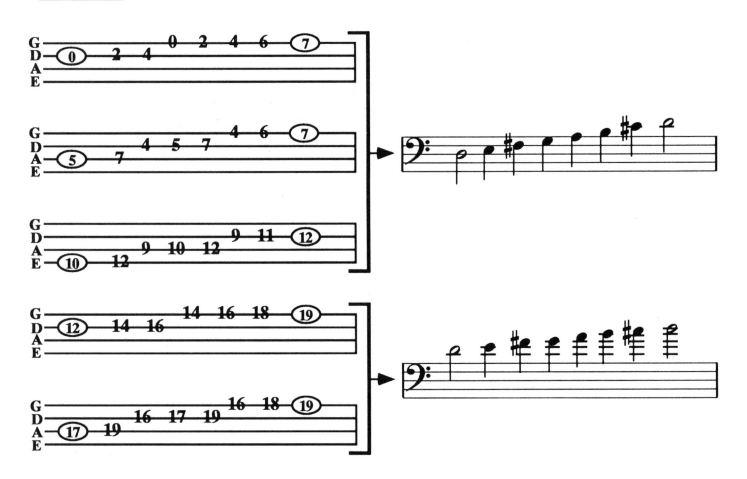

Riff

22

E MAJOR SCALE

FORMULA - (E) Root (F#) 2nd (G#) 3rd (A) 4th (B) 5th (C#) 6th (D#) 7th

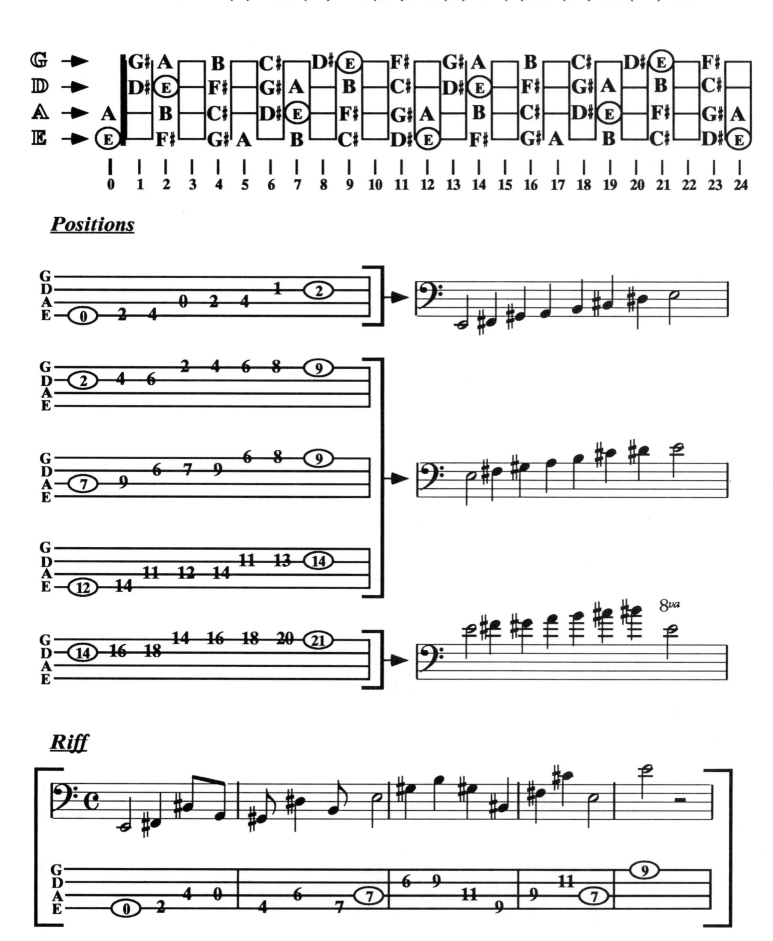

23

F MAJOR SCALE

FORMULA - (F) Root (G) 2nd (A) 3rd (B♭) 4th (C) 5th (D) 6th (E) 7th

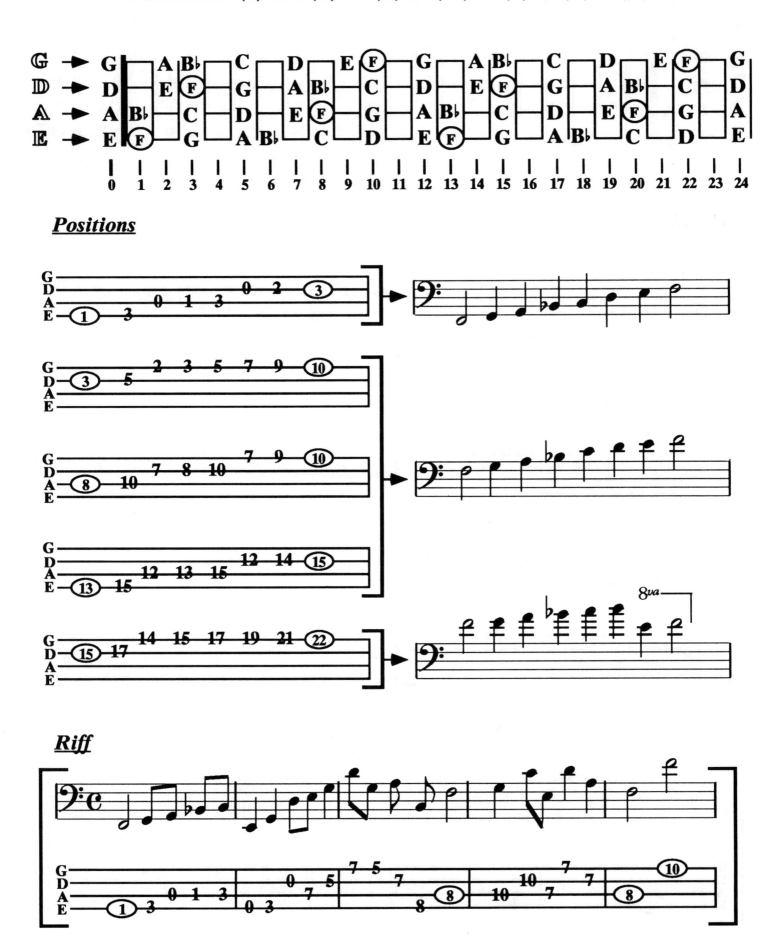

24

G MAJOR SCALE
FORMULA - (G) Root (A) 2nd (B) 3rd (C) 4th (D) 5th (E) 6th (F♯) 7th

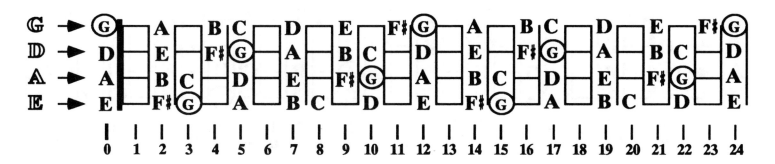

Positions

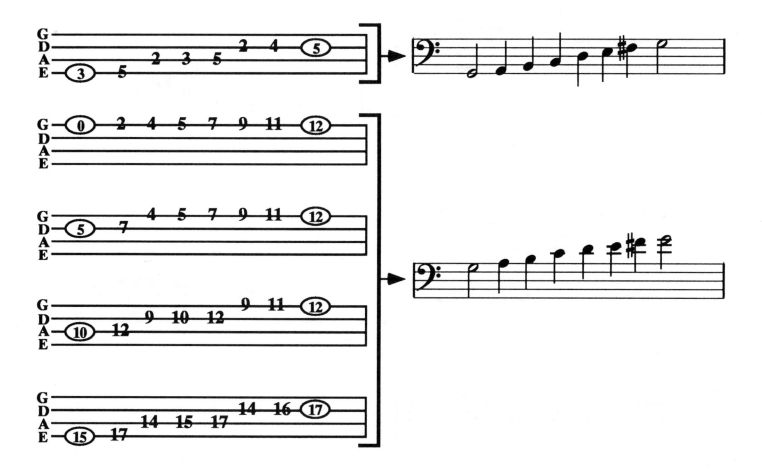

Riff

25

A MAJOR SCALE
FORMULA - (A) Root (B) 2nd (C♯) 3rd (D) 4th (E) 5th (F♯) 6th (G♯) 7th

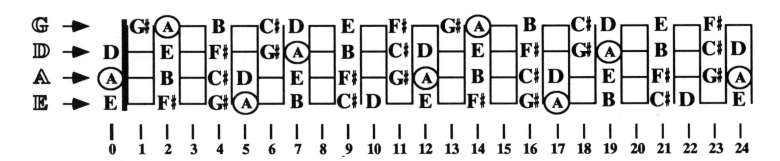

Positions

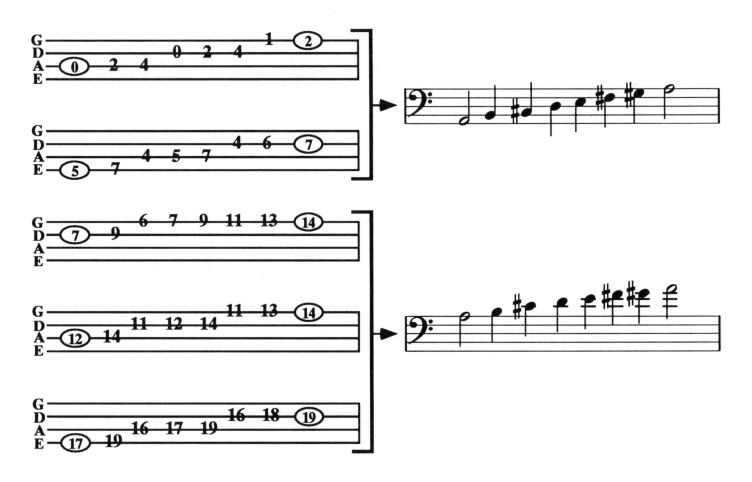

Riff

26

B MAJOR SCALE
FORMULA - (B) Root (C♯) 2nd (D♯) 3rd (E) 4th (F♯) 5th (G♯) 6th (A♯) 7th

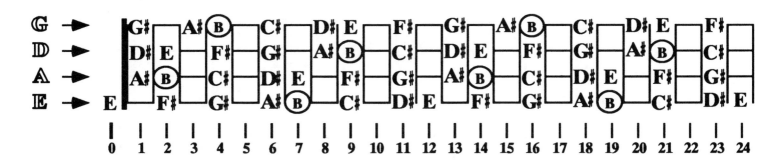

Positions

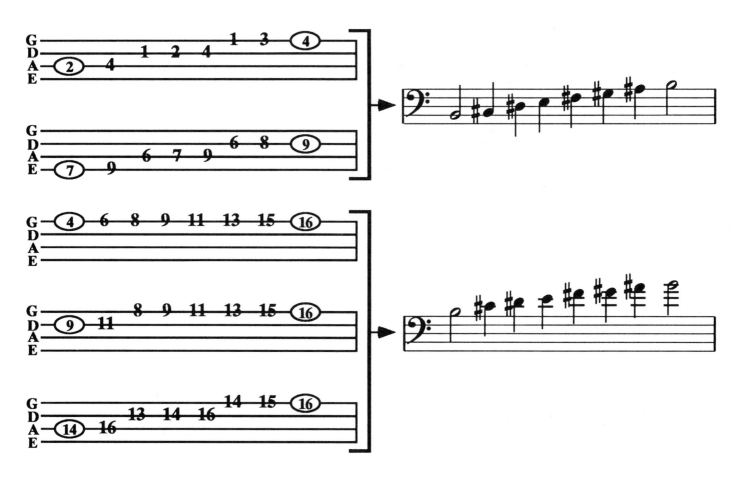

Riff

C MINOR SCALE
FORMULA - (C) Root (D) 2nd (E♭) ♭3rd (F) 4th (G) 5th (A♭) ♭6th (B♭) ♭7th

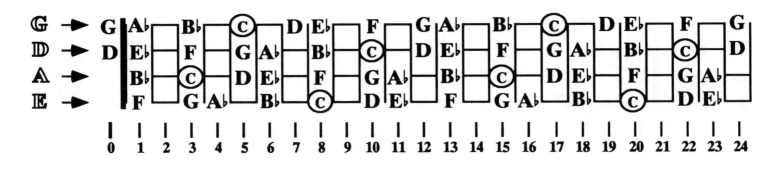

Positions

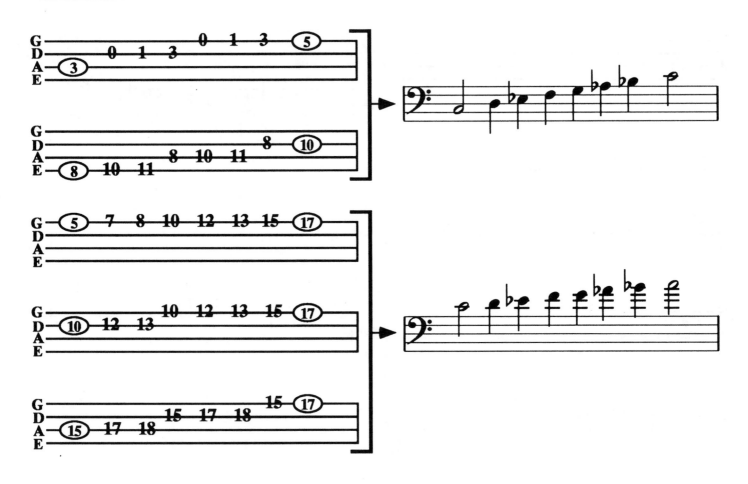

Riff

28

D MINOR SCALE
FORMULA - (D) Root (E) 2nd (F)♭3rd (G) 4th (A) 5th (B♭)♭6th (C)♭7th

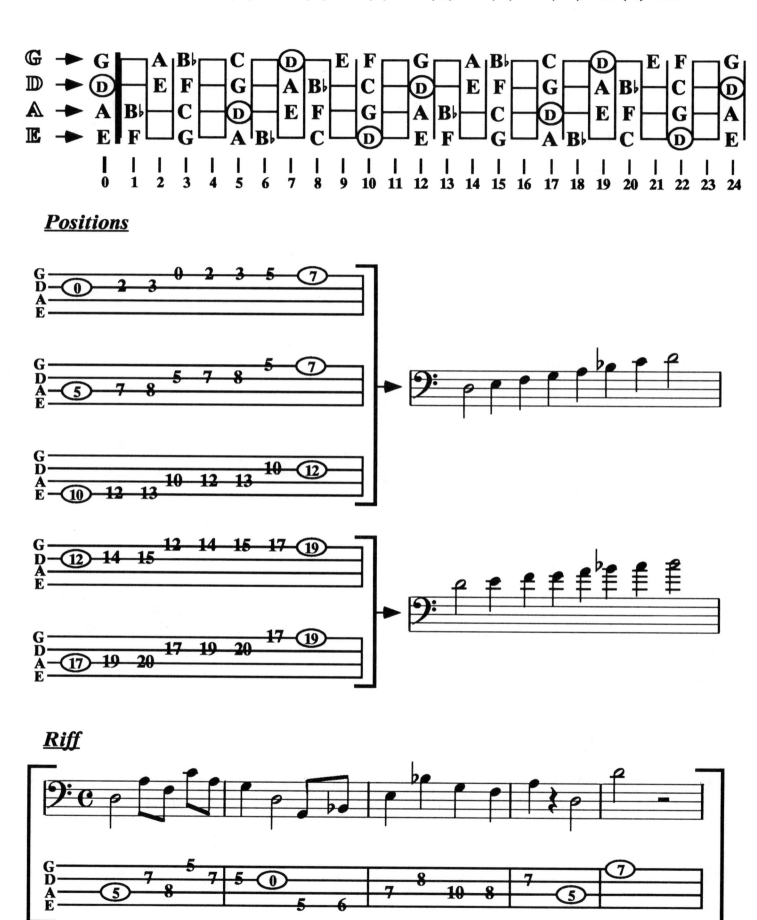

E MINOR SCALE
FORMULA - (E) Root (F♯) 2nd (G) ♭3rd (A) 4th (B) 5th (C) ♭6th (D) ♭7th

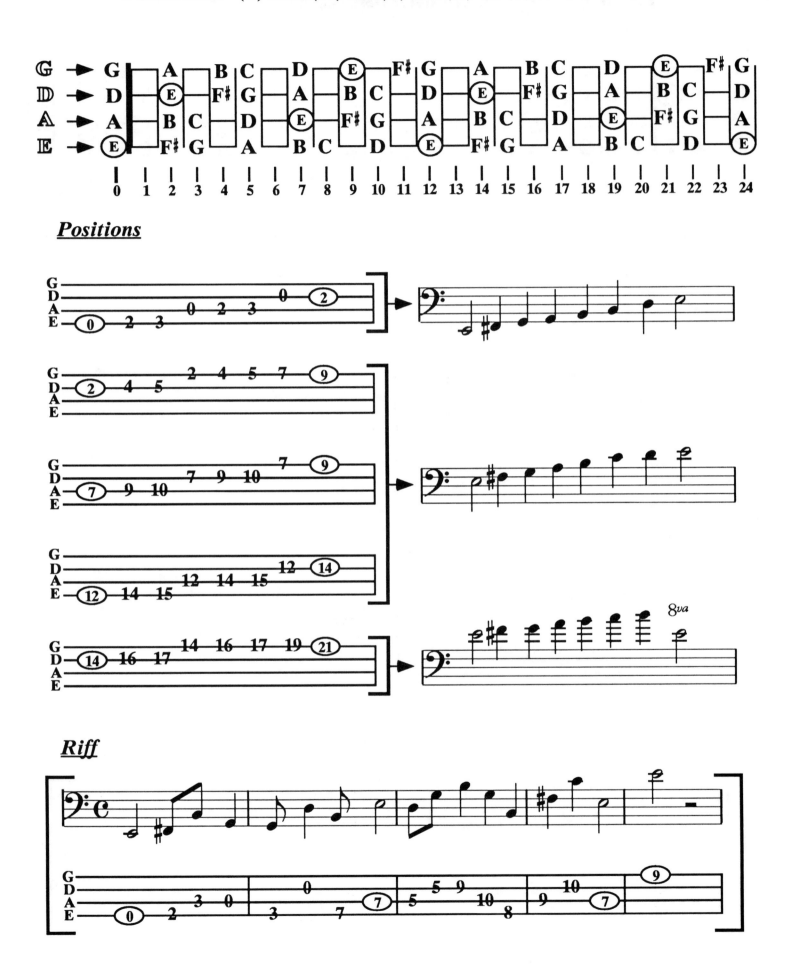

F MINOR SCALE
FORMULA - (F) Root (G) 2nd (A♭) ♭3rd (B♭) 4th (C) 5th (D♭) ♭6th (E♭) ♭7th

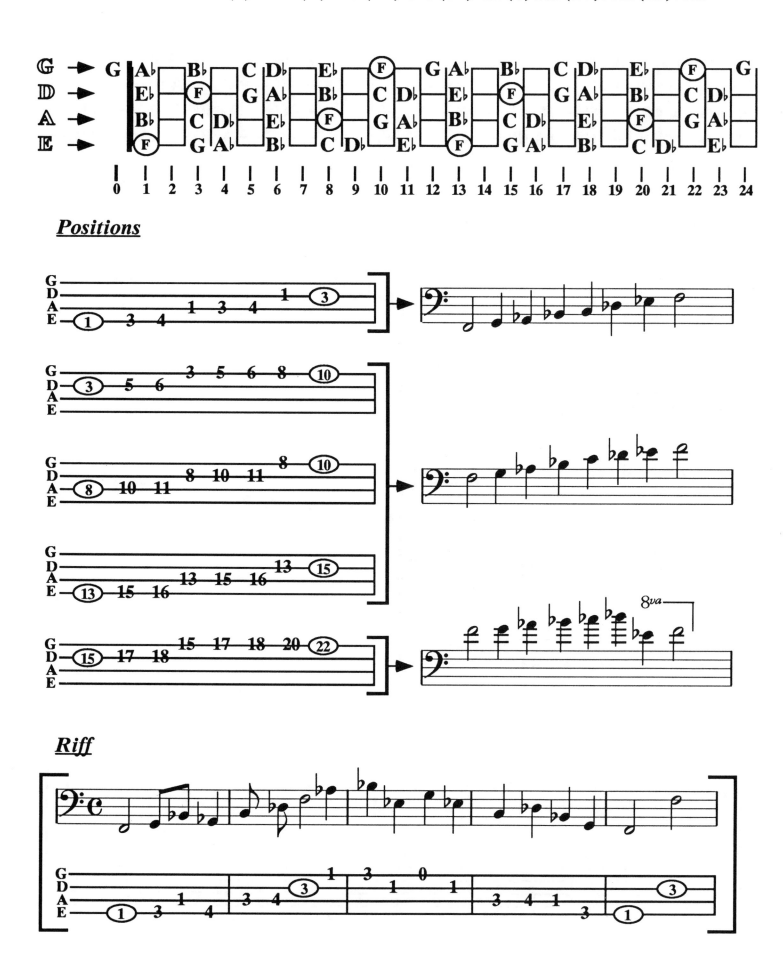

Positions

Riff

G MINOR SCALE
FORMULA - (G) Root (A) 2nd (B♭) ♭3rd (C) 4th (D) 5th (E♭) ♭6th (F) ♭7th

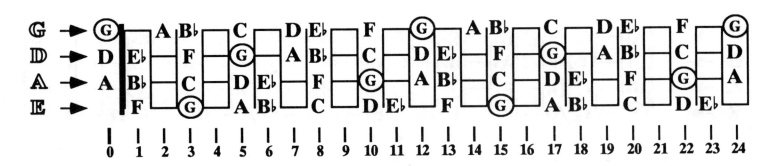

Positions

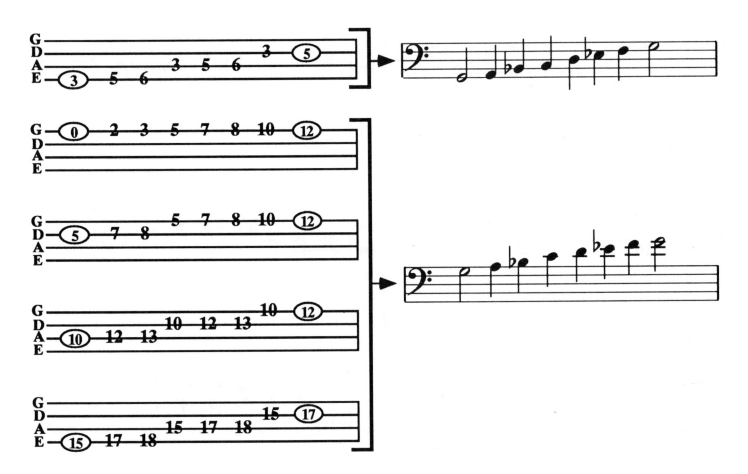

Riff

A MINOR SCALE
FORMULA - (A) Root (B) 2nd (C) ♭3rd (D) 4th (E) 5th (F) ♭6th (G) ♭7th

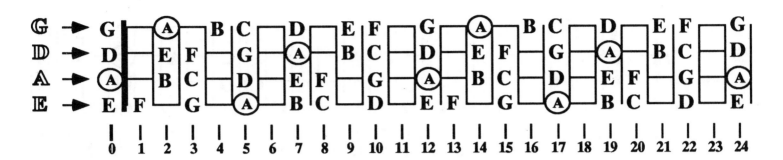

Positions

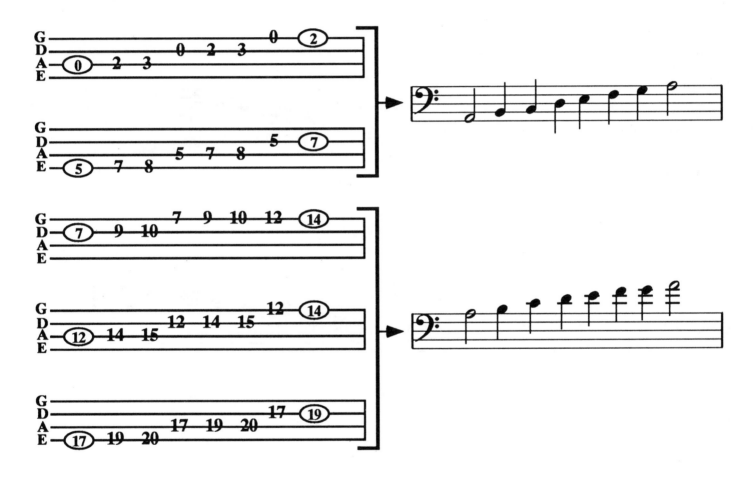

Riff

33

B MINOR SCALE
FORMULA - (B) Root (C#) 2nd (D) ♭3rd (E) 4th (F#) 5th (G)♭6th (A) ♭7th

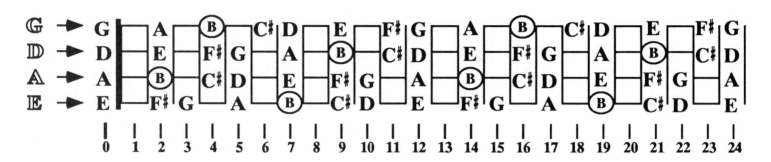

Positions

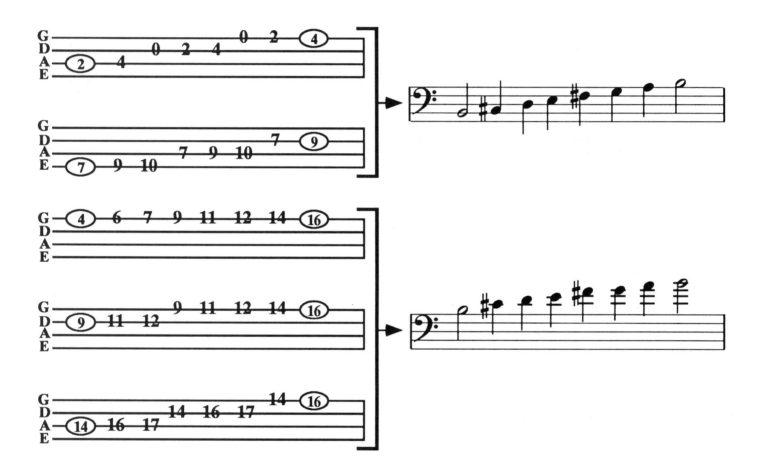

Riff

C MAJOR PENTATONIC
FORMULA - (C) Root (D) 2nd (E) 3rd (G) 5th (A) 6th

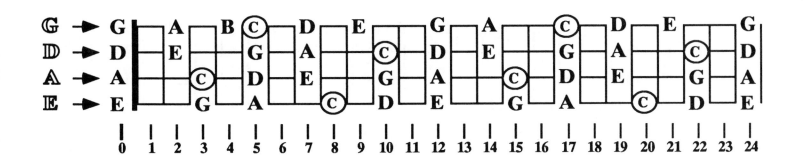

Positions

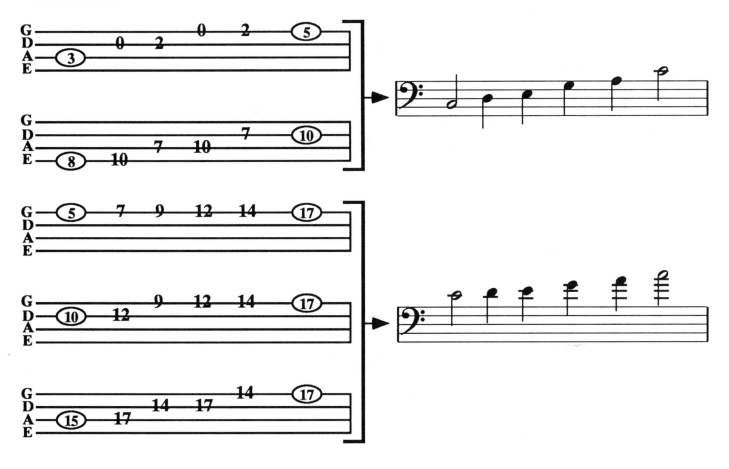

Riff

D MAJOR PENTATONIC
FORMULA - (D) Root (E) 2nd (F#) 3rd (A) 5th (B) 6th

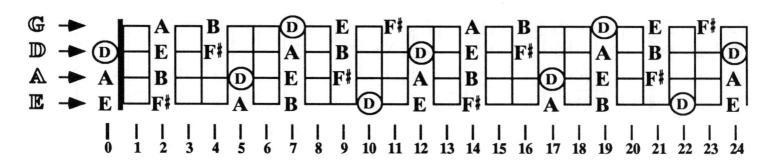

Positions

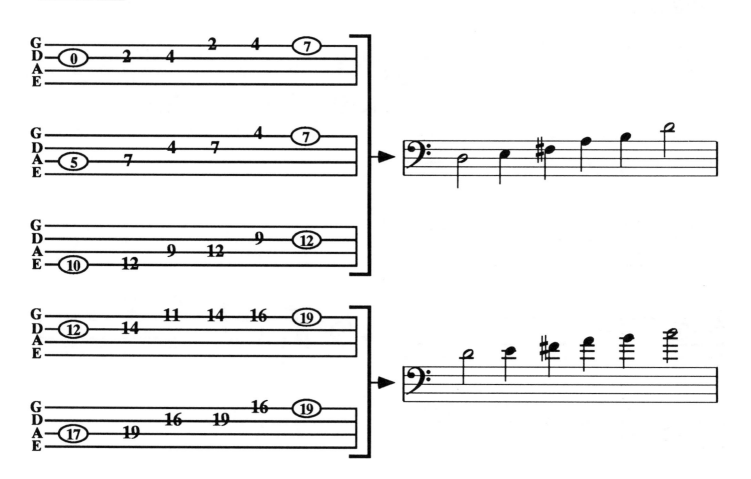

Riff

36

E MAJOR PENTATONIC
FORMULA - (E) Root (F#) 2nd (G#) 3rd (B) 5th (C#) 6th

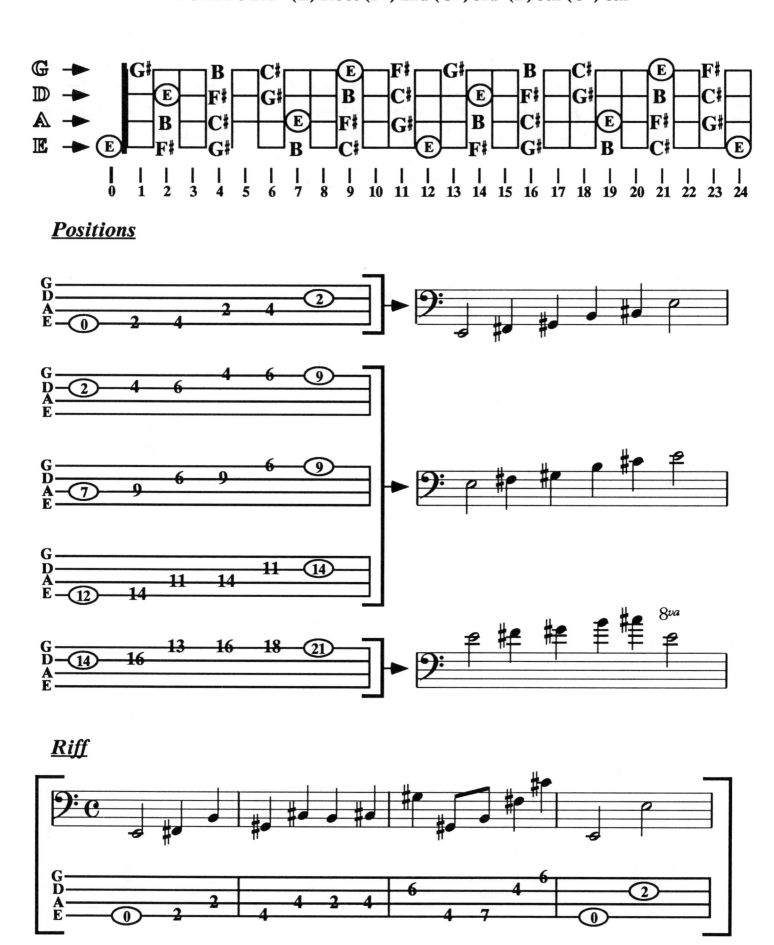

Positions

Riff

F MAJOR PENTATONIC
FORMULA - (F) Root (G) 2nd (A) 3rd (C) 5th (D) 6th

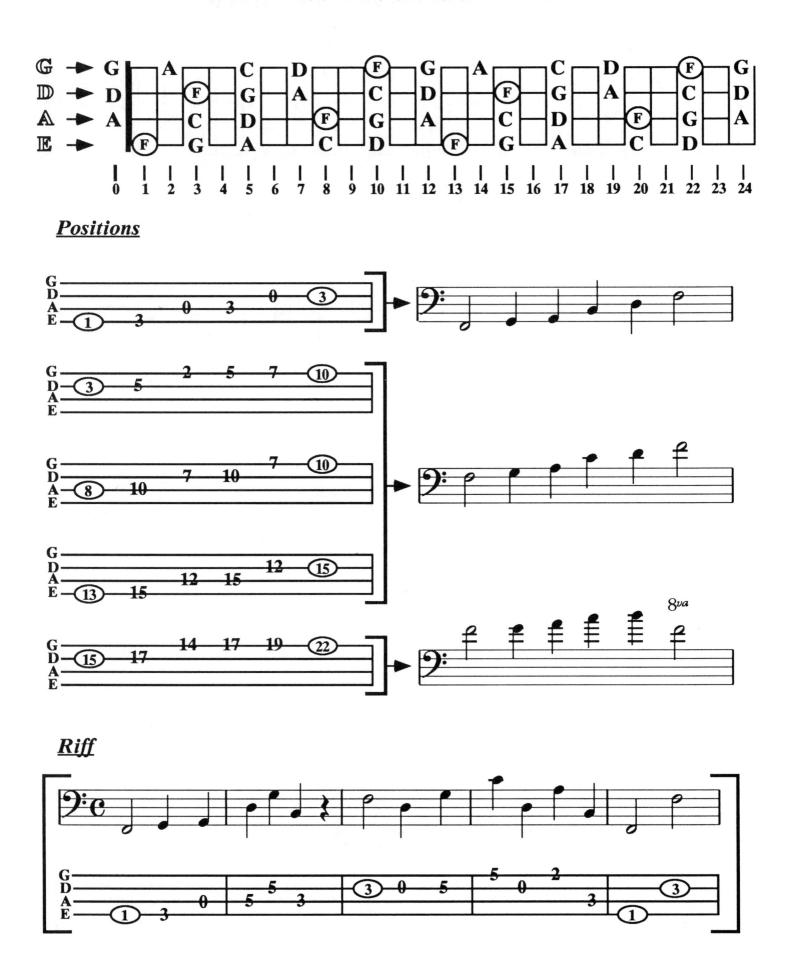

Positions

Riff

38

G MAJOR PENTATONIC
FORMULA - (G) Root (A) 2nd (B) 3rd (D) 5th (E) 6th

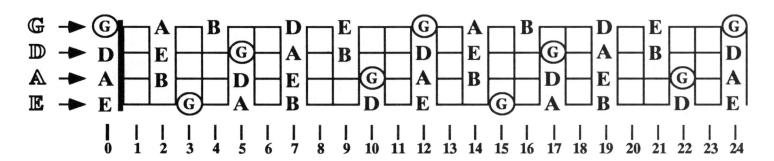

Positions

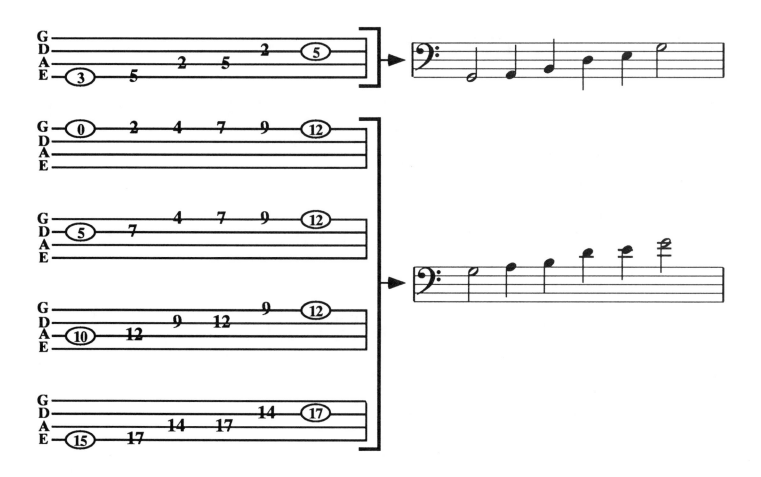

Riff

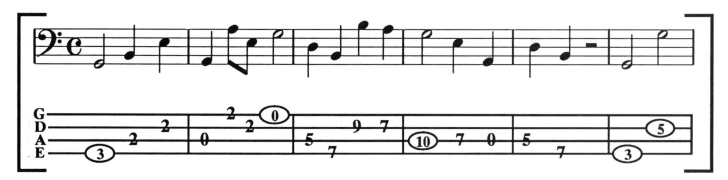

39

A MAJOR PENTATONIC
FORMULA - (A) Root (B) 2nd (C#) 3rd (E) 5th (F#) 6th

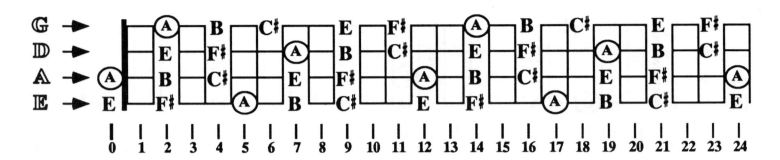

Positions

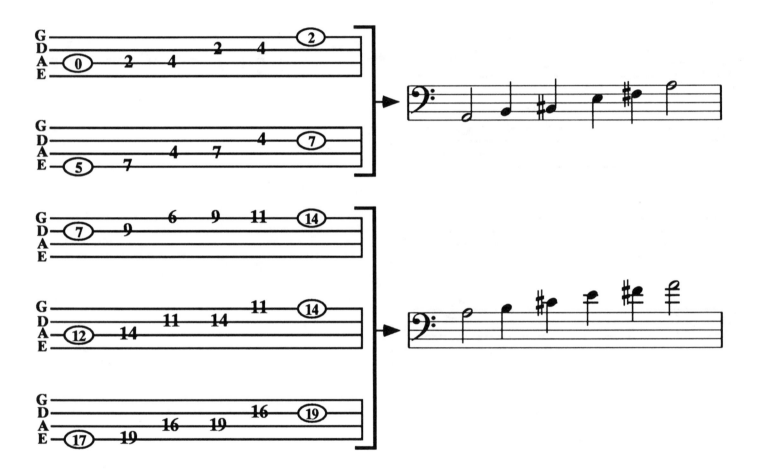

Riff

B MAJOR PENTATONIC
FORMULA - (B) Root (C#) 2nd (D#) 3rd (F#) 5th (G#) 6th

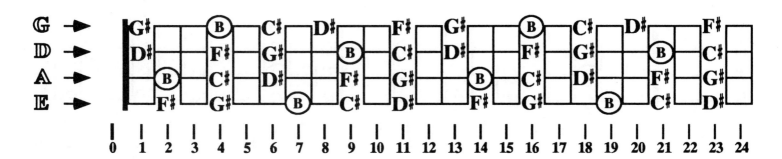

Positions

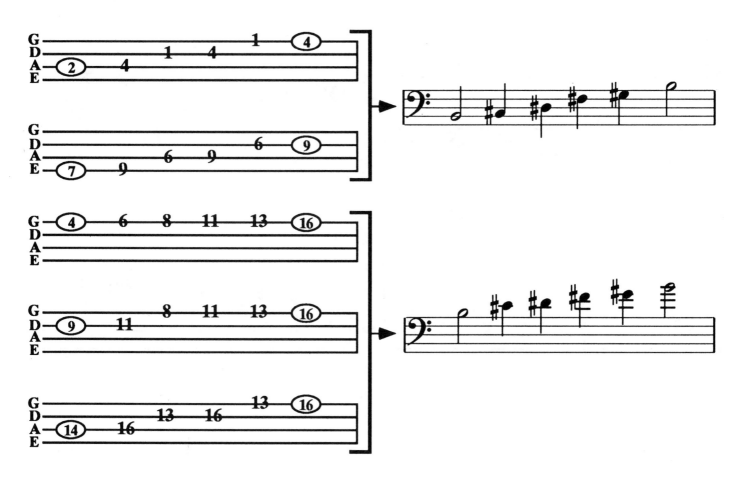

Riff

C MINOR PENTATONIC
FORMULA - (C) Root (E♭) ♭3rd (F) 4th (G) 5th (B♭) ♭7th

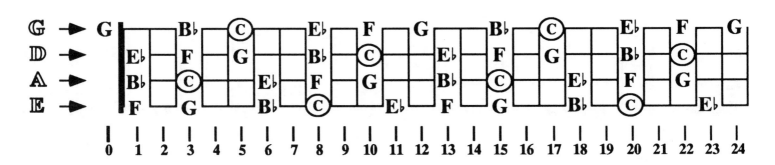

Positions

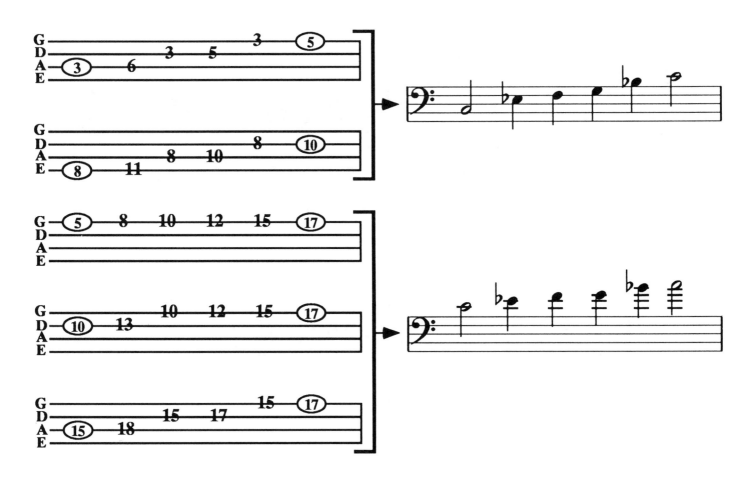

Riff

D MINOR PENTATONIC
FORMULA - (D) Root (F) ♭3rd (G) 4th (A) 5th (C) ♭7th

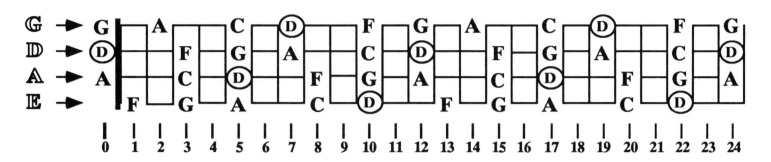

Positions

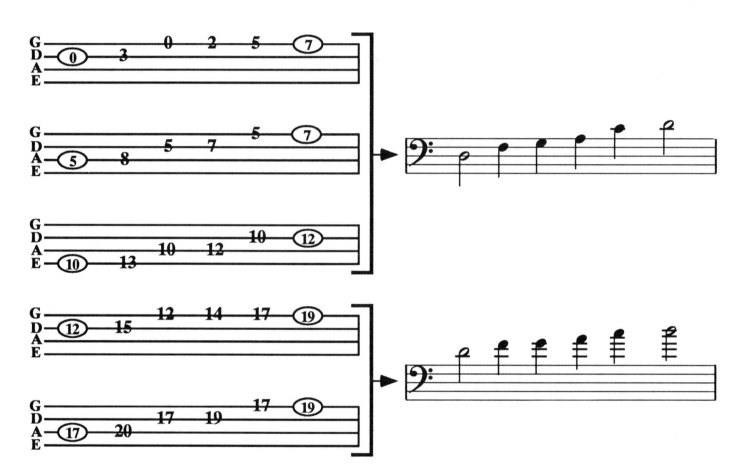

Riff

E MINOR PENTATONIC
FORMULA - (E) Root (G) ♭3rd (A) 4th (B) 5th (D) ♭7th

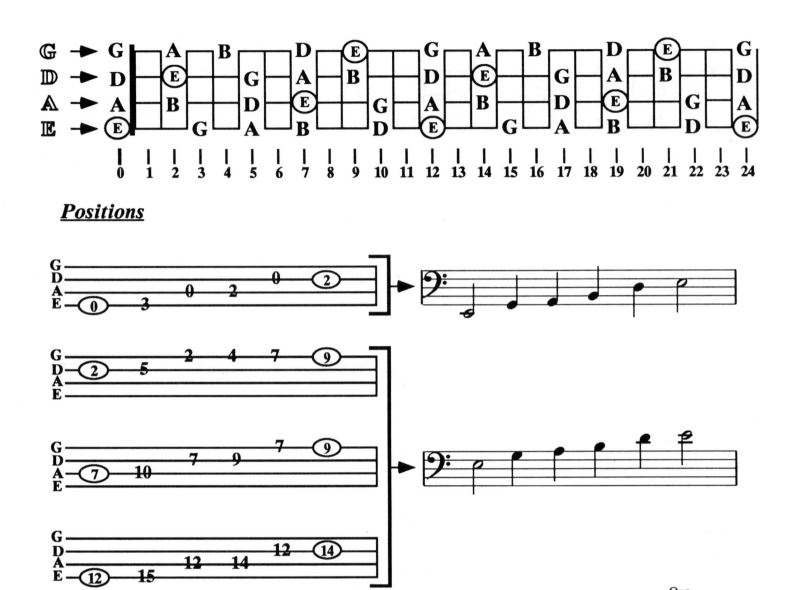

Positions

Riff

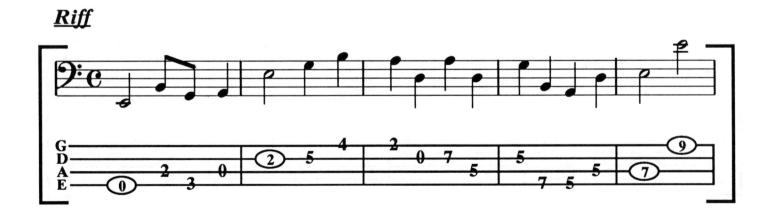

F MINOR PENTATONIC
FORMULA - (F) Root (A♭) ♭3rd (B♭) 4th (C) 5th (E♭) ♭7th

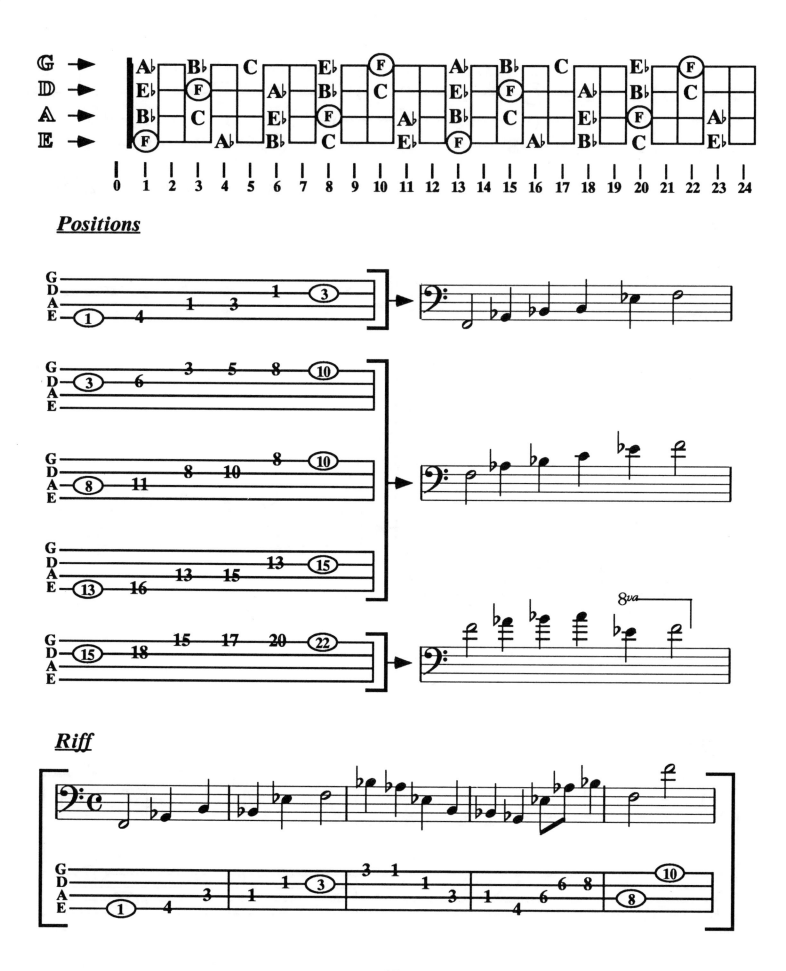

Positions

Riff

G MINOR PENTATONIC
FORMULA - (G) Root (B♭) ♭3rd (C) 4th (D) 5th (F) ♭7th

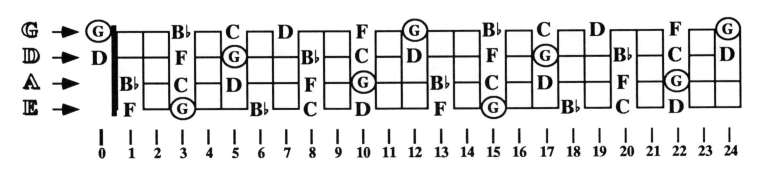

Positions

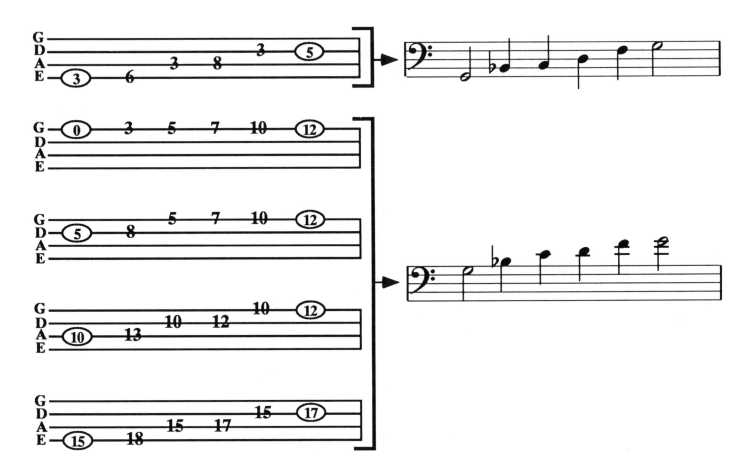

Riff

46

A MINOR PENTATONIC
FORMULA - (A) Root (C) ♭3rd (D) 4th (E) 5th (G) ♭7th

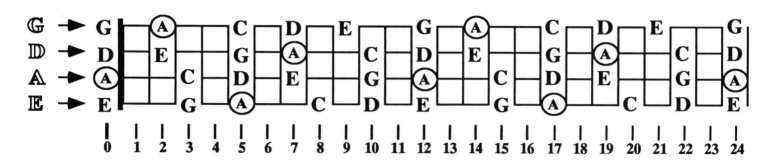

Positions

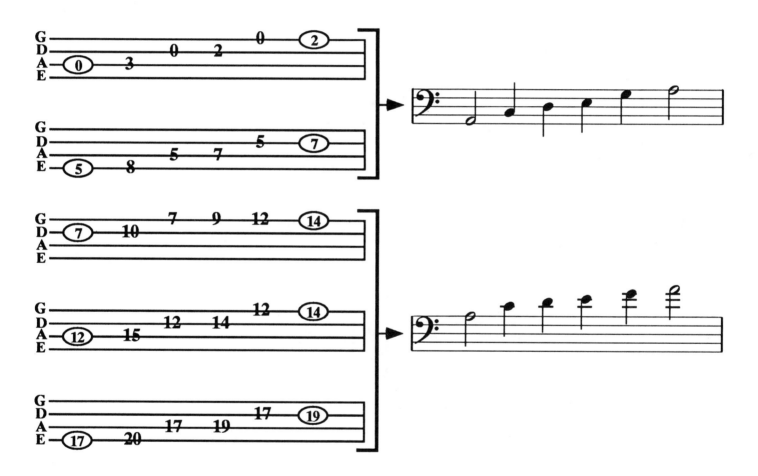

Riff

B MINOR PENTATONIC
FORMULA - (B) Root (D) ♭3rd (E) 4th (F♯) 5th (A) ♭7th

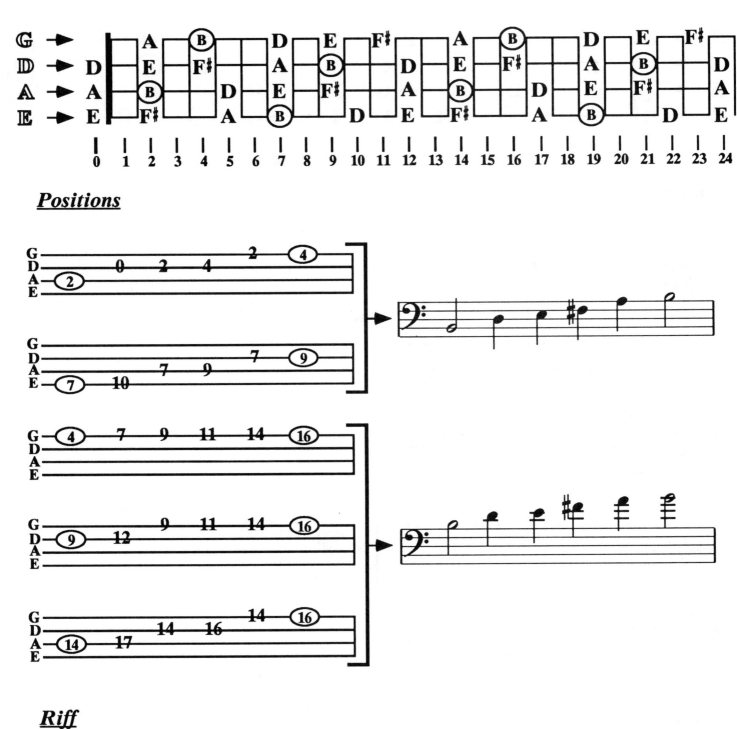

Positions

Riff

C BLUES SCALE
FORMULA - (C) Root (E♭) ♭3rd (F) 4th (G♭) ♭5th (A♯) ♮6th (B♭) ♭7th

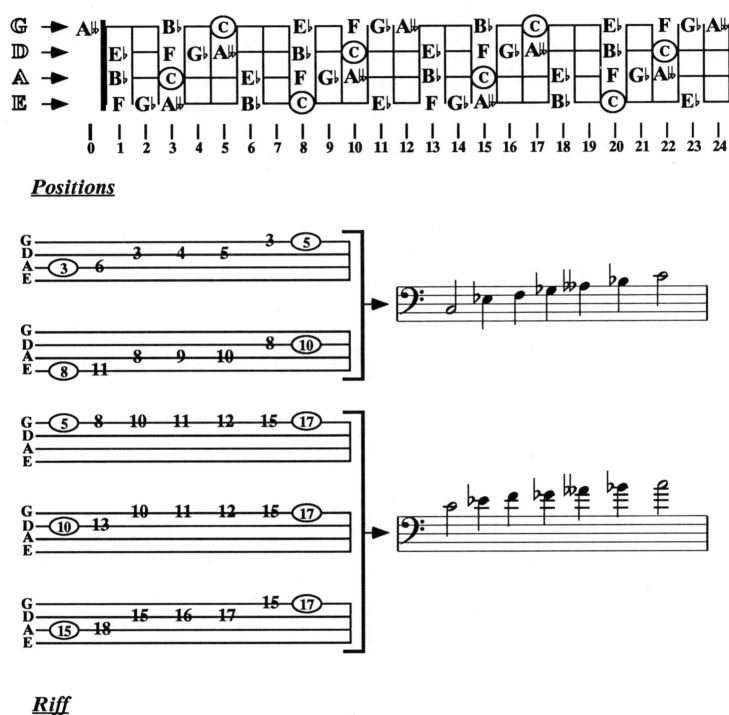

Positions

Riff

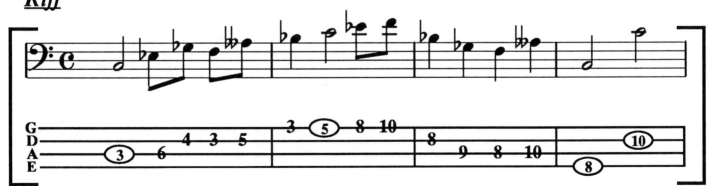

D BLUES SCALE
FORMULA - (D) Root (F) ♭3rd (G) 4th (A♭) ♭5th (B♭♭) ♭♭6th (C) ♭7th

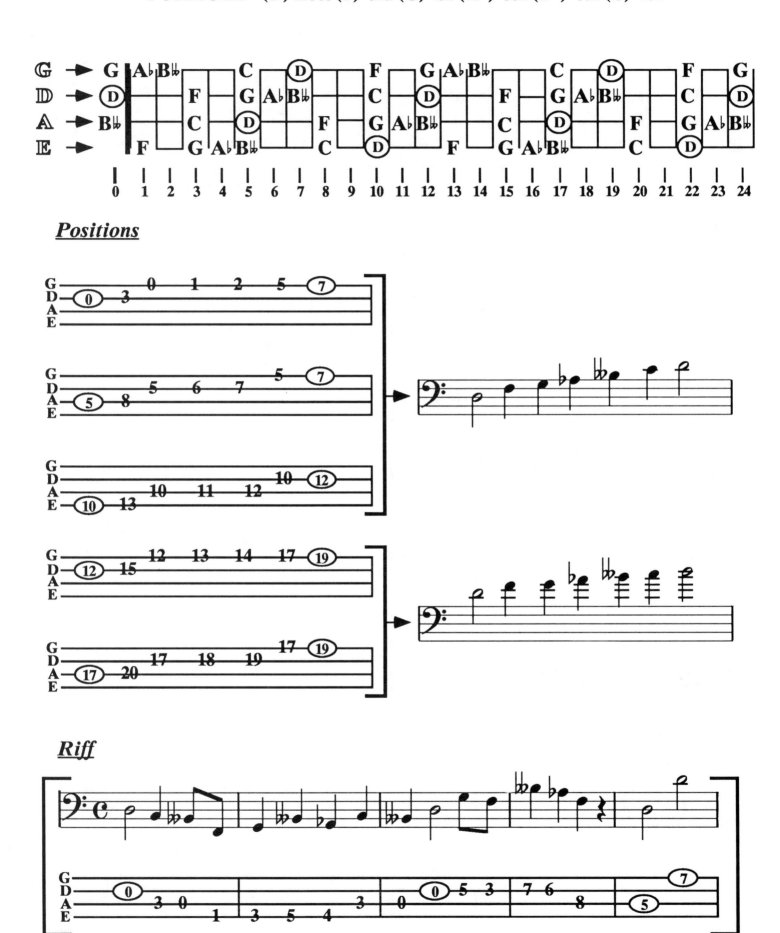

Positions

Riff

E BLUES SCALE
FORMULA - (E) Root (G) ♭3rd (A) 4th (B♭) ♭5th (C♭)♮6th (D) ♭7th

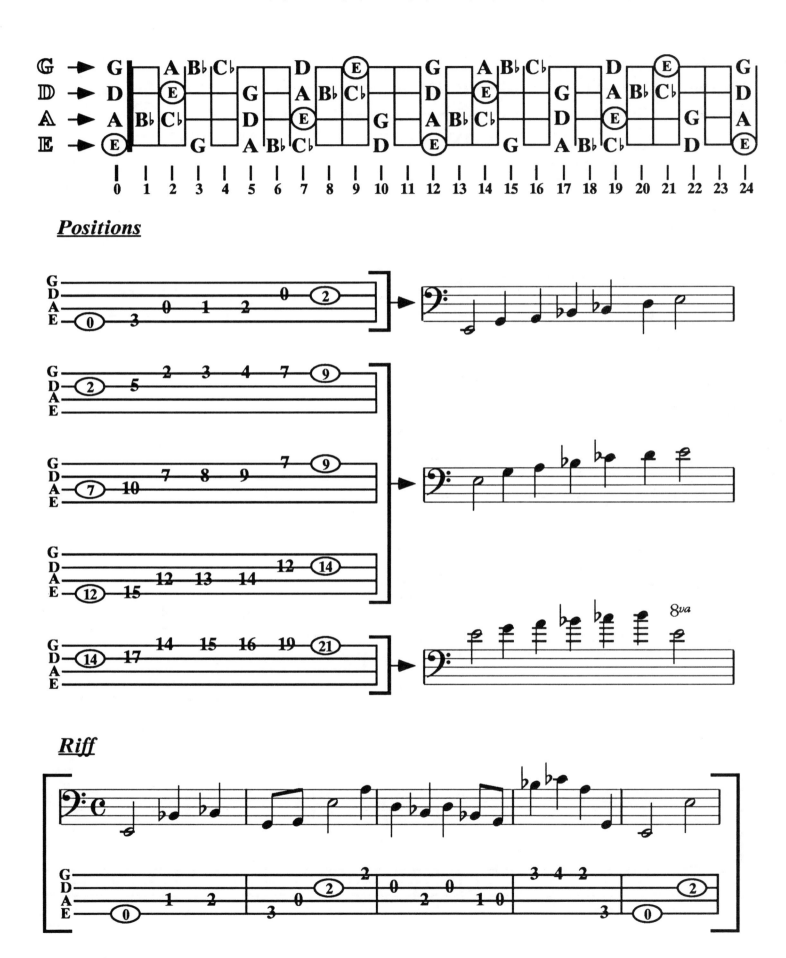

51

F BLUES SCALE
FORMULA - (F) Root (A♭) ♭3rd (B♭) 4th (C♭) ♭5th (D♮) ♮6th (E♭) ♭7th

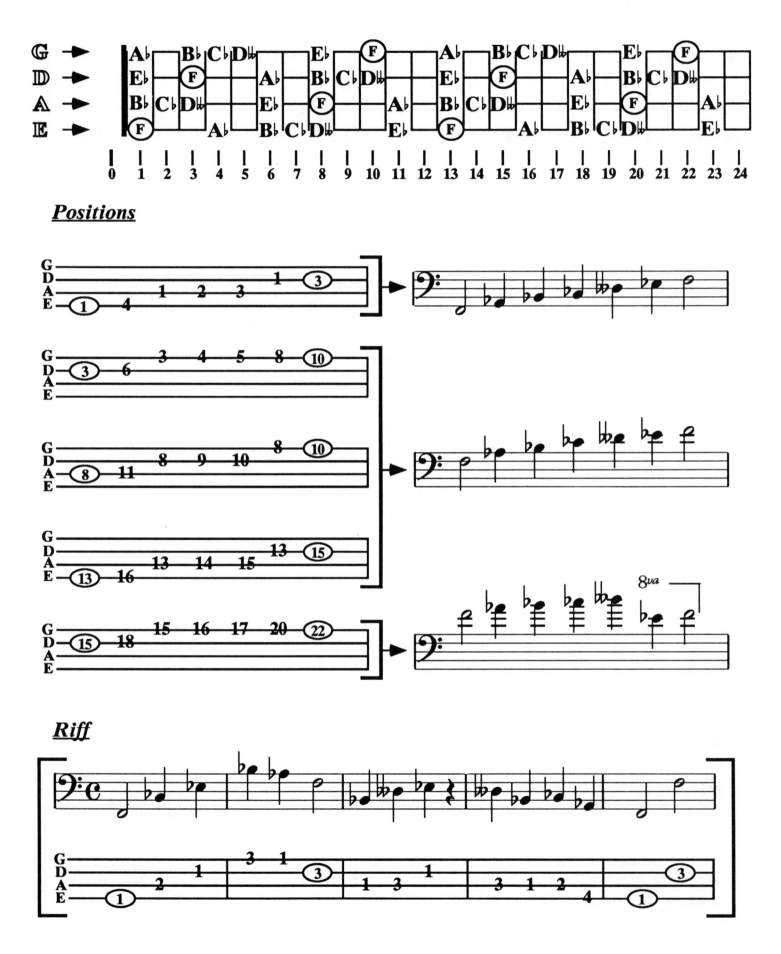

52

G BLUES SCALE
FORMULA - (G) Root (B♭) ♭3rd (C) 4th (D♭) ♭5th (E♮) ♮6th (F) ♭7th

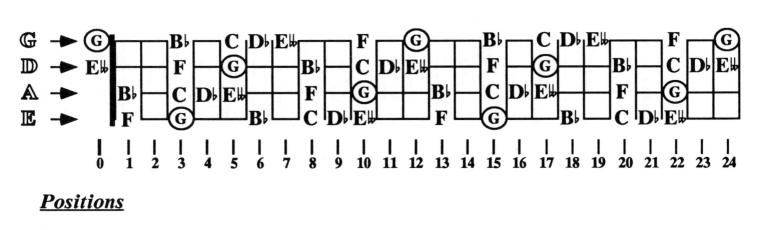

Positions

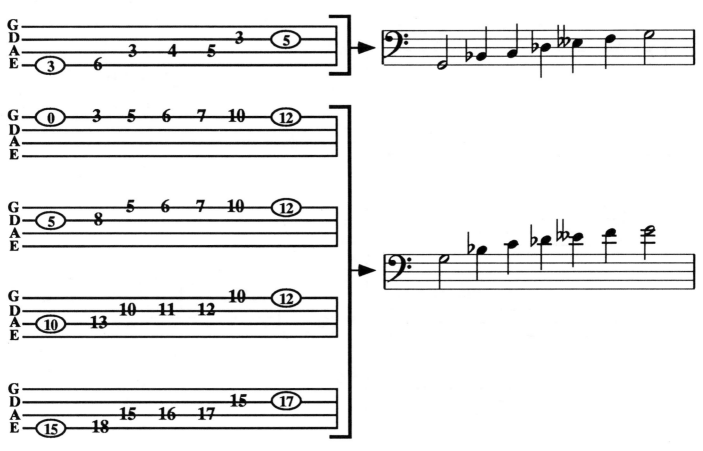

Riff

A BLUES SCALE
FORMULA - (A) Root (C) ♭3rd (D) 4th (E♭) ♭5th (F♭) ♮6th (G) ♭7th

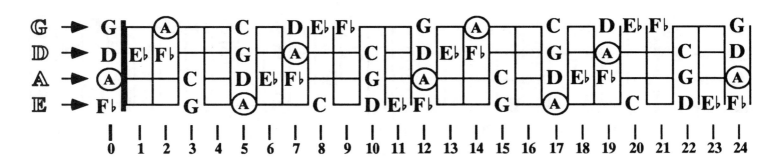

Positions

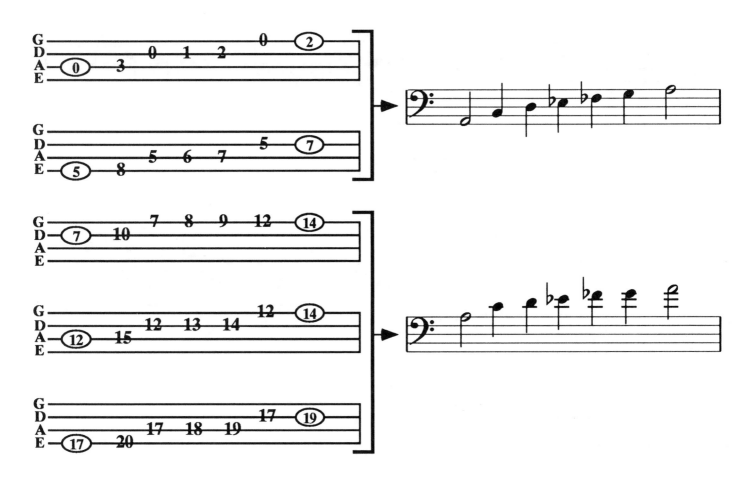

Riff

54

B BLUES SCALE

FORMULA - (B) Root (D) ♭3rd (E) 4th (F) ♭5th (G♭)♮6th (A) ♭7th

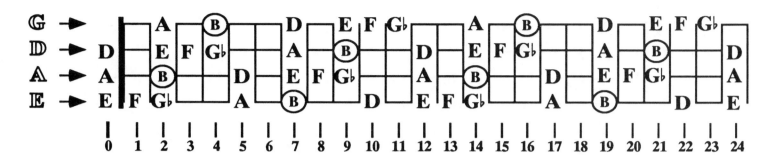

Positions

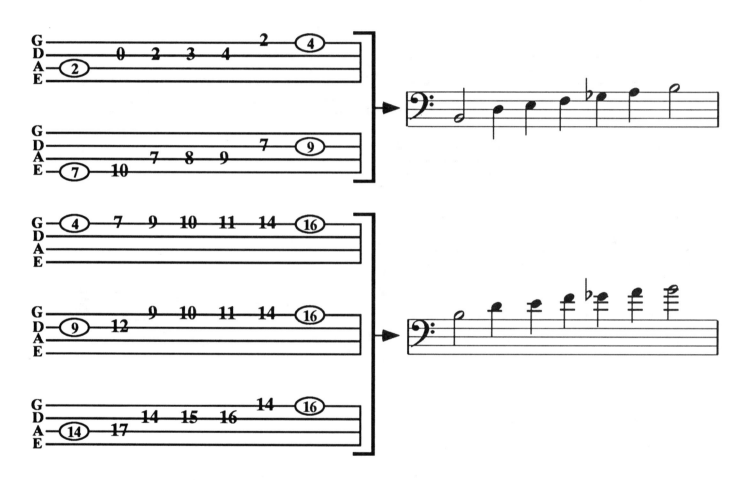

Riff

C MIXOLYDIAN MODE
FORMULA - (C) Root (D) 2nd (E) 3rd (F) 4th (G) 5th (A) 6th (B♭) ♭7th

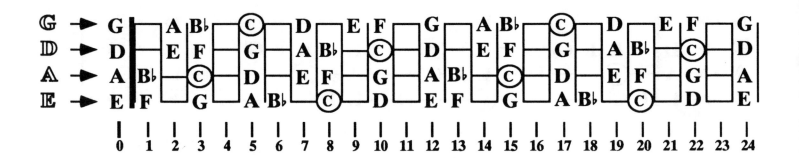

Positions

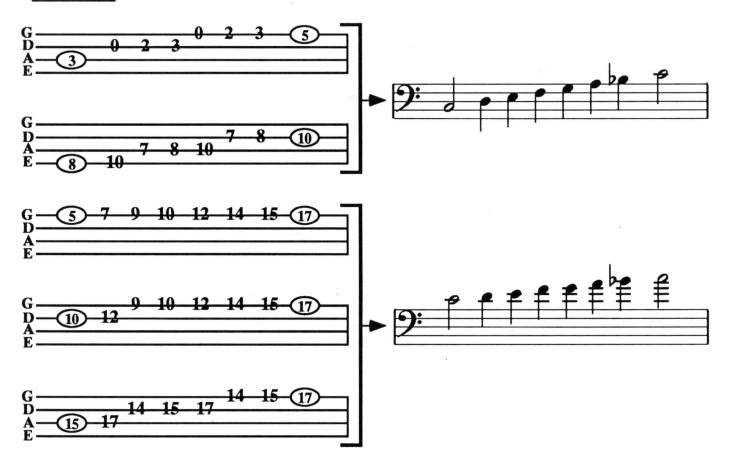

Riff

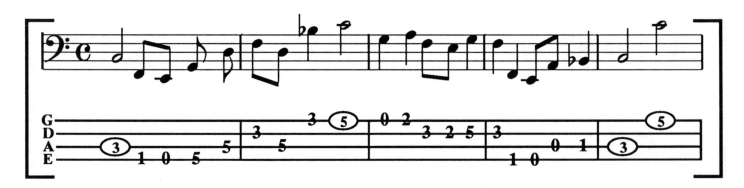

56

D MIXOLYDIAN MODE
FORMULA - (D) Root (E) 2nd (F♯) 3rd (G) 4th (A) 5th (B) 6th (C) ♭7th

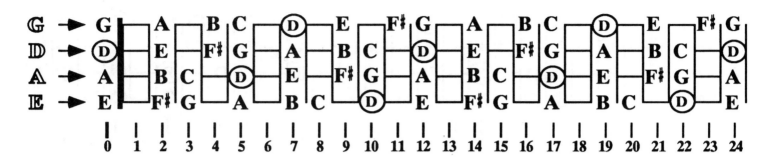

Positions

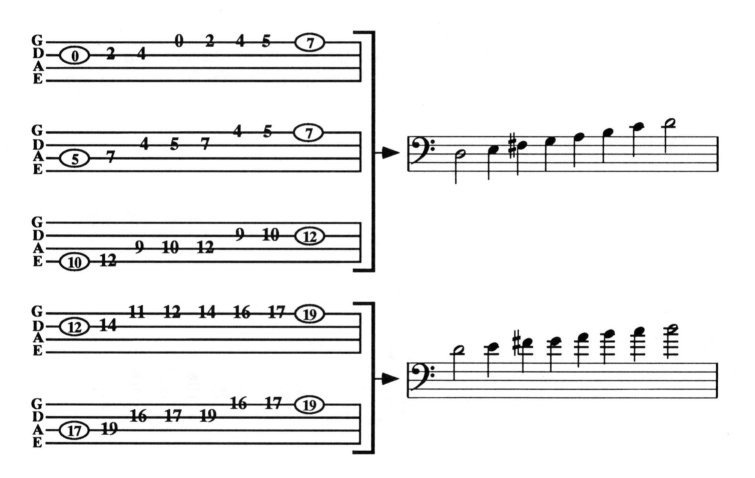

Riff

E MIXOLYDIAN MODE
FORMULA - (E) Root (F#) 2nd (G#) 3rd (A) 4th (B) 5th (C#) 6th (D) ♭7th

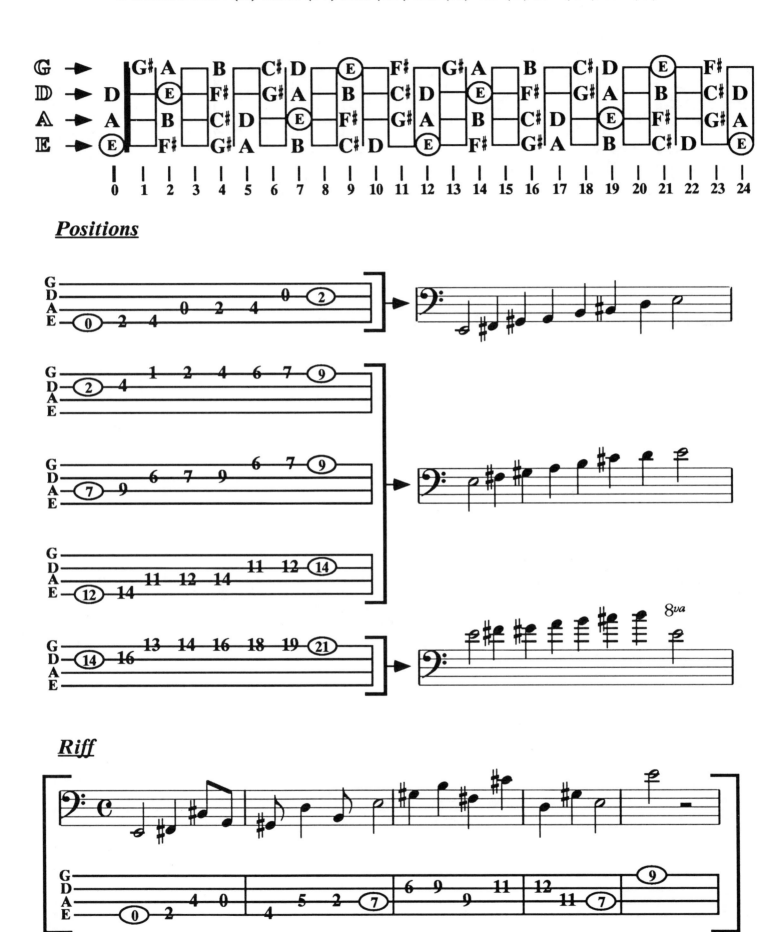

Positions

Riff

F MIXOLYDIAN MODE
FORMULA - (F) Root (G) 2nd (A) 3rd (B♭) 4th (C) 5th (D) 6th (E♭) ♭7th

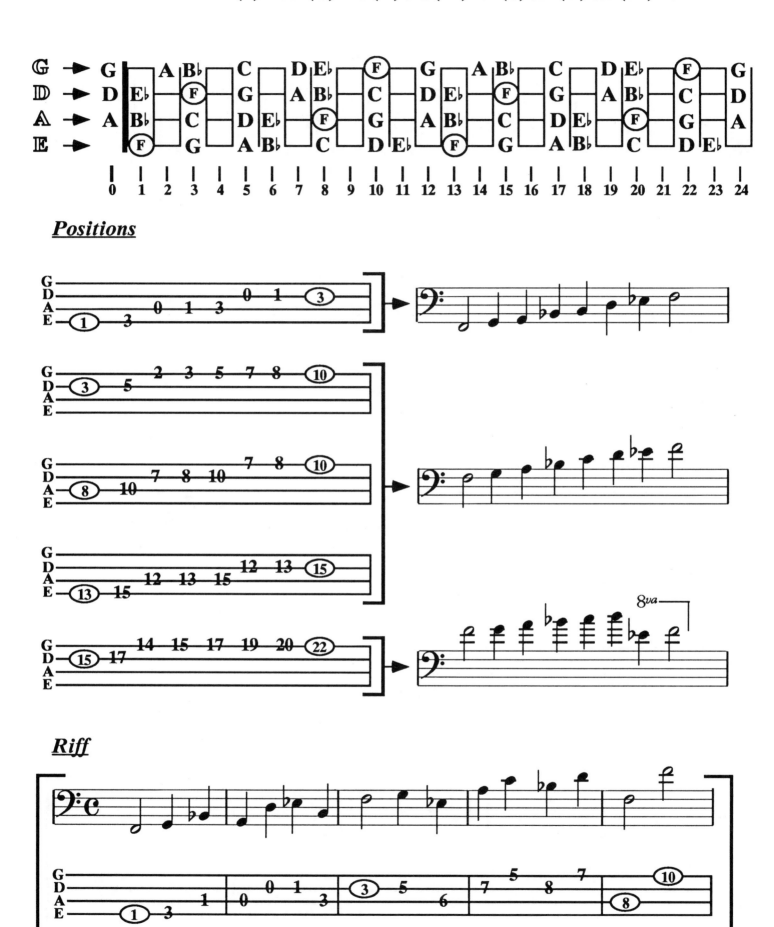

Positions

Riff

G MIXOLYDIAN MODE
FORMULA - (G) Root (A) 2nd (B) 3rd (C) 4th (D) 5th (E) 6th (F) ♭7th

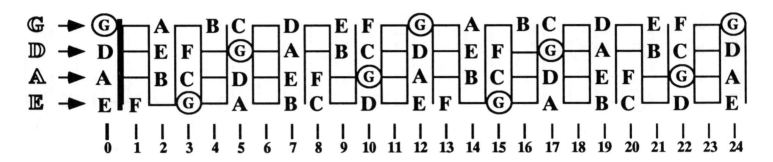

Positions

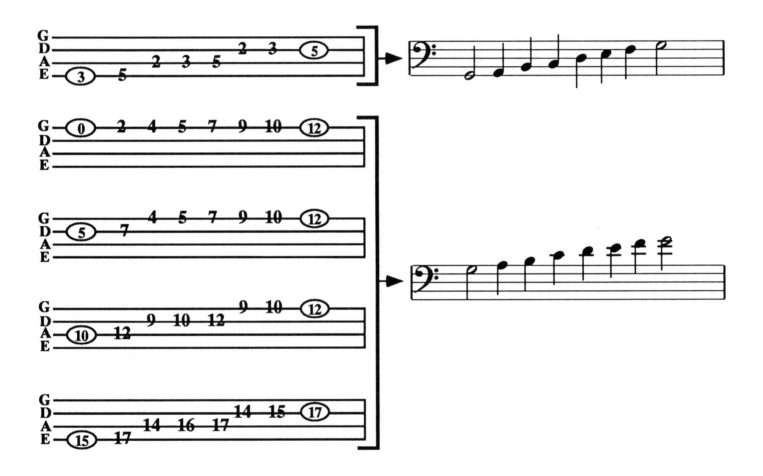

Riff

A MIXOLYDIAN MODE
FORMULA - (A) Root (B) 2nd (C♯) 3rd (D) 4th (E) 5th (F♯) 6th (G) ♭7th

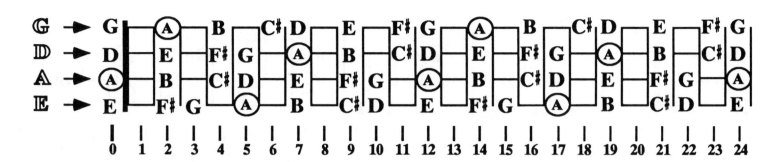

Positions

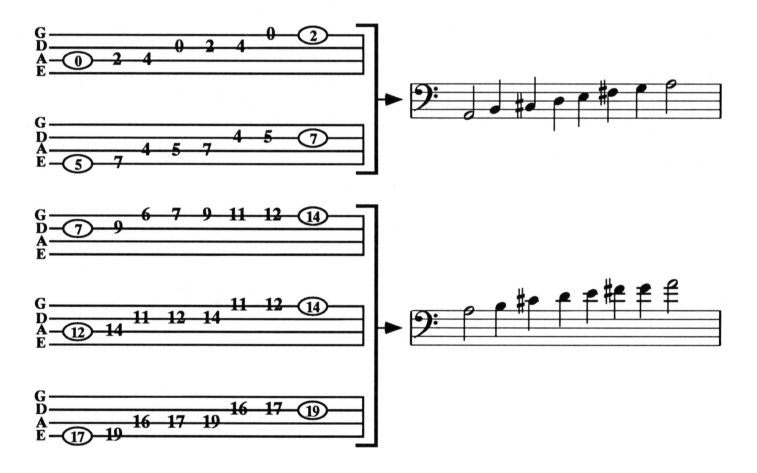

Riff

B   MIXOLYDIAN MODE
FORMULA - (B) Root (C♯) 2nd (D♯) 3rd (E) 4th (F♯) 5th (G♯) 6th (A) ♭7th

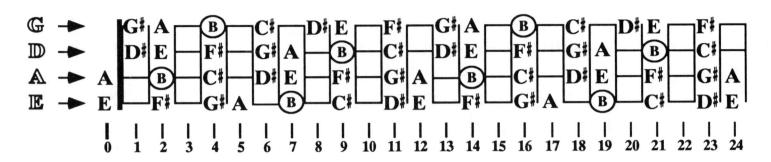

Positions

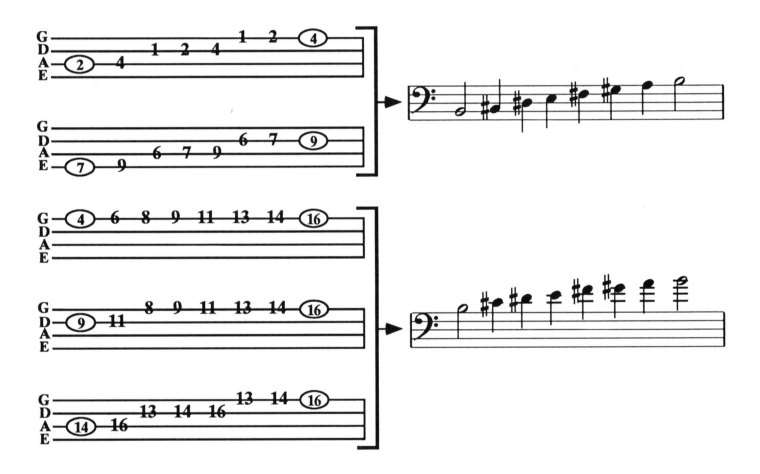

Riff

C DORIAN MODE
FORMULA - (C) Root (D) 2nd (E♭) ♭3rd (F) 4th (G) 5th (A) 6th (B♭) ♭7th

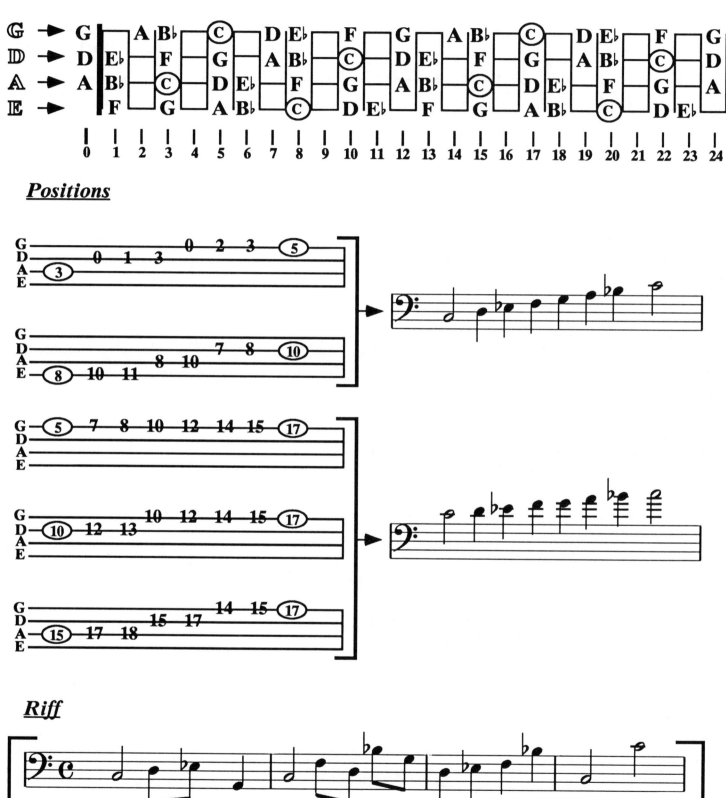

Positions

Riff

D DORIAN MODE
FORMULA - (D) Root (E) 2nd (F) ♭3rd (G) 4th (A) 5th (B) 6th (C) ♭7th

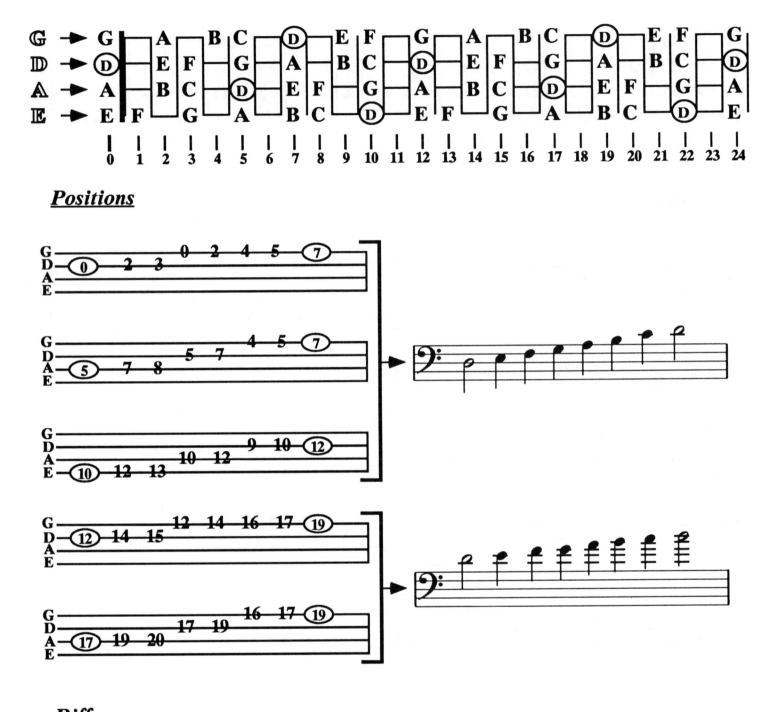

Positions

Riff

E DORIAN MODE
FORMULA - (E) Root (F#) 2nd (G) b3rd (A) 4th (B) 5th (C#) 6th (D) b7th

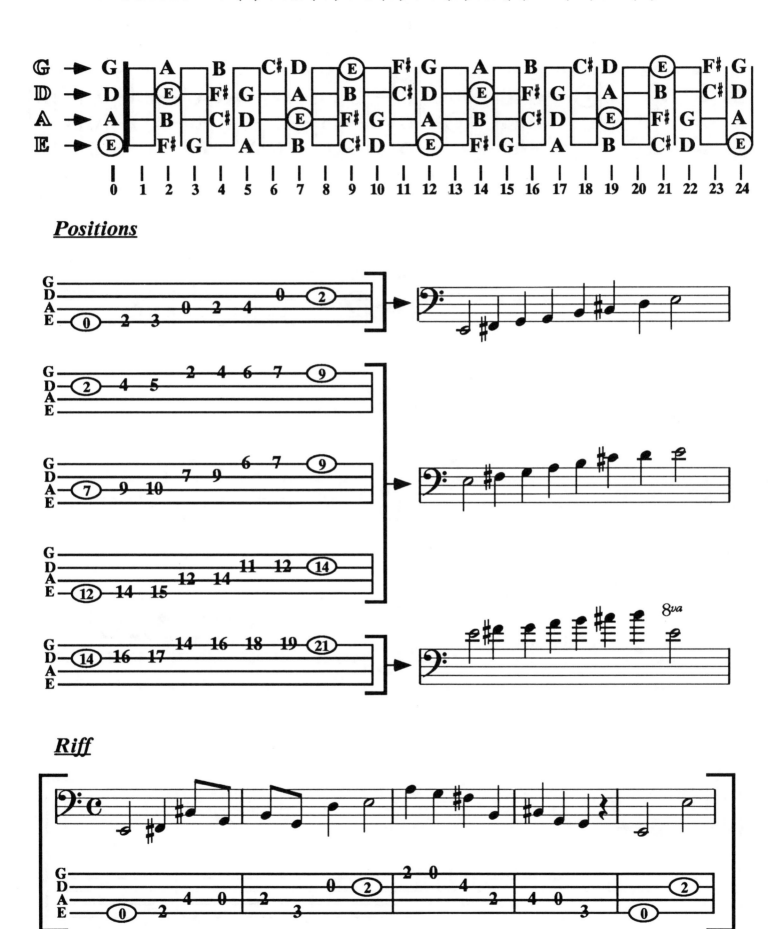

Positions

Riff

F DORIAN MODE
FORMULA - (F) Root (G) 2nd (A♭) ♭3rd (B♭) 4th (C) 5th (D) 6th (E♭) ♭7th

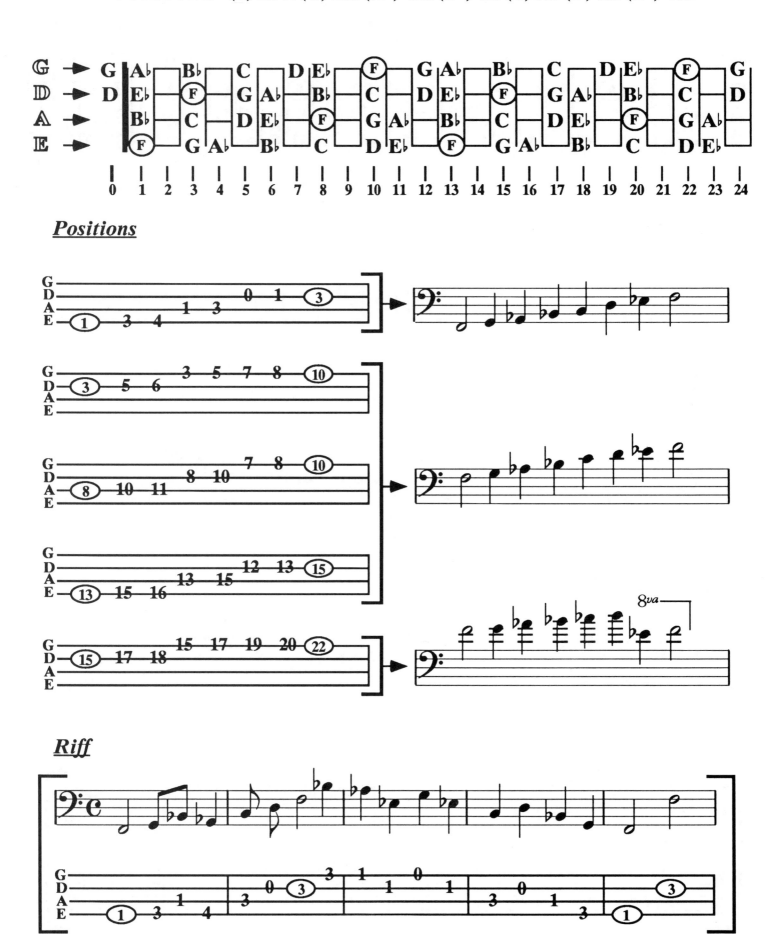

Positions

Riff

G DORIAN MODE
FORMULA - (G) Root (A) 2nd (B♭) ♭3rd (C) 4th (D) 5th (E) 6th (F) ♭7th

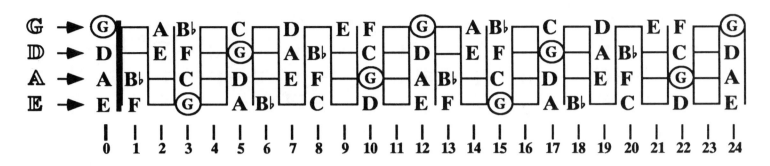

Positions

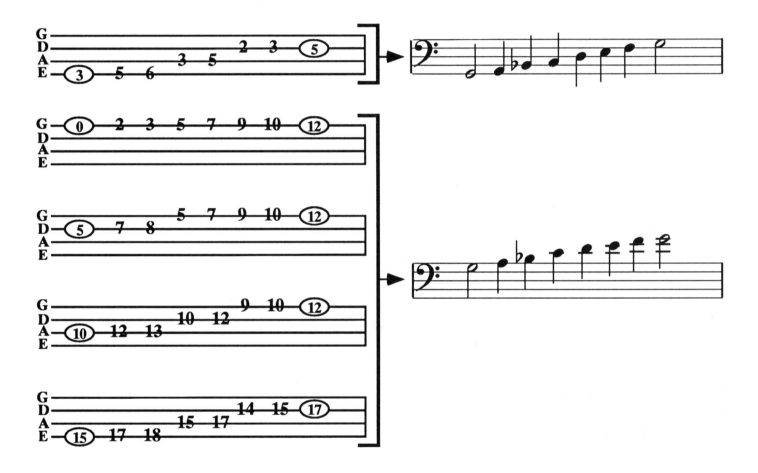

Riff

A DORIAN MODE
FORMULA - (A) Root (B) 2nd (C) ♭3rd (D) 4th (E) 5th (F♯) 6th (G) ♭7th

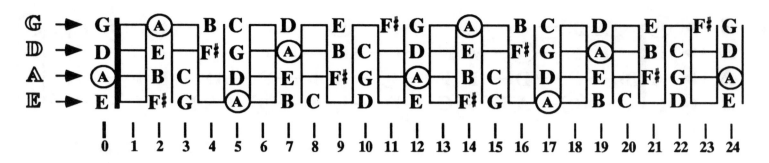

Positions

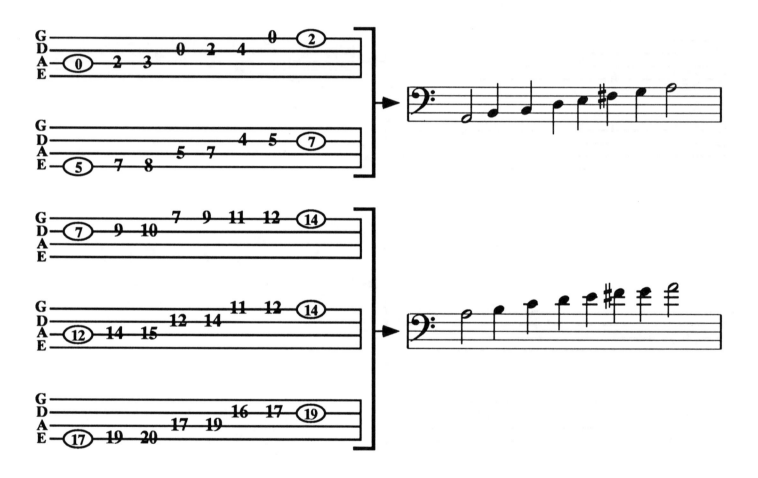

Riff

B DORIAN MODE
FORMULA - (B) Root (C#) 2nd (D) ♭3rd (E) 4th (F#) 5th (G#) 6th (A) ♭7th

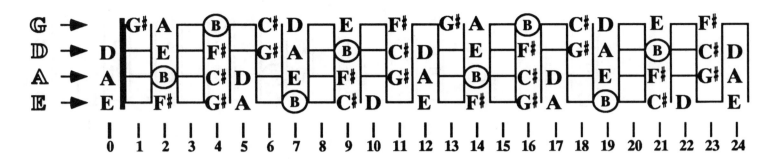

Positions

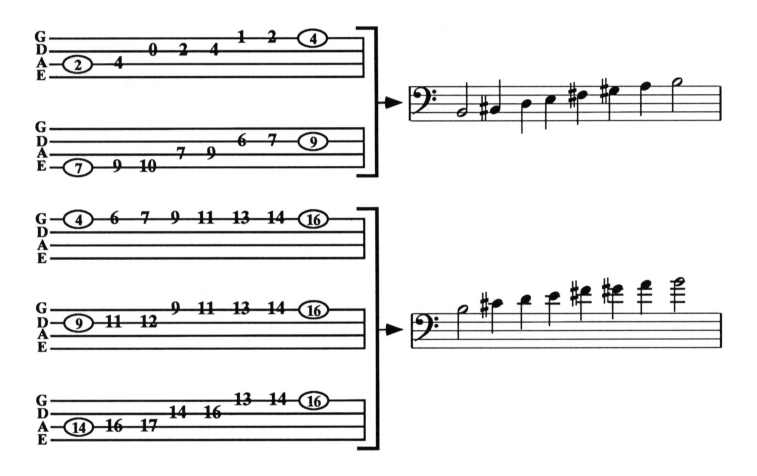

Riff

C LYDIAN MODE
FORMULA - (C) Root (D) 2nd (E) 3rd (F#) #4th (G) 5th (A) 6th (B) 7th

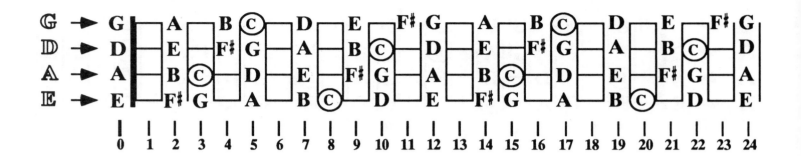

Positions

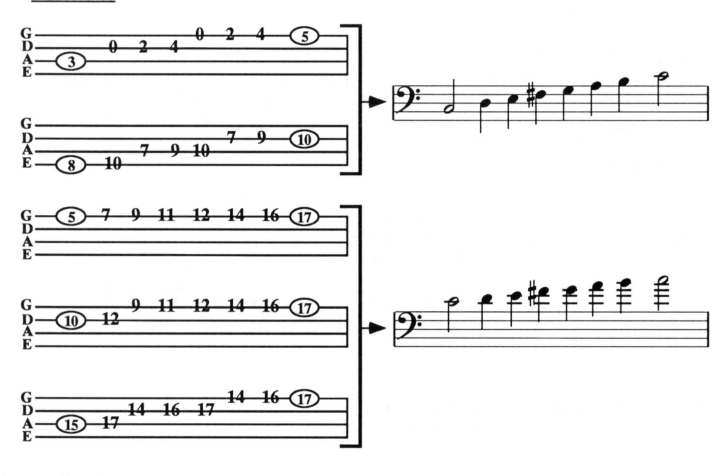

Riff

70

D LYDIAN MODE
FORMULA - (D) Root (E) 2nd (F♯) 3rd (G♯) ♯4th (A) 5th (B) 6th (C♯) 7th

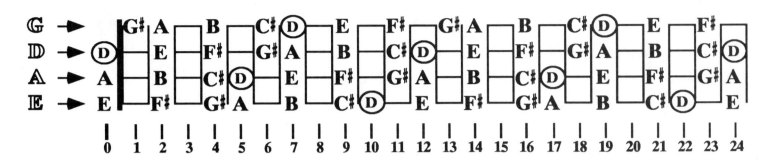

Positions

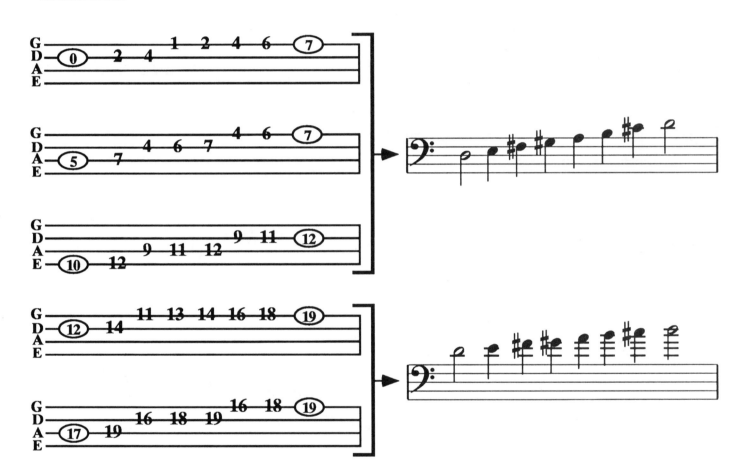

Riff

71

E LYDIAN MODE
FORMULA - (E) Root (F♯) 2nd (G♯) 3rd (A♯) ♯4th (B) 5th (C♯) 6th (D♯) 7th

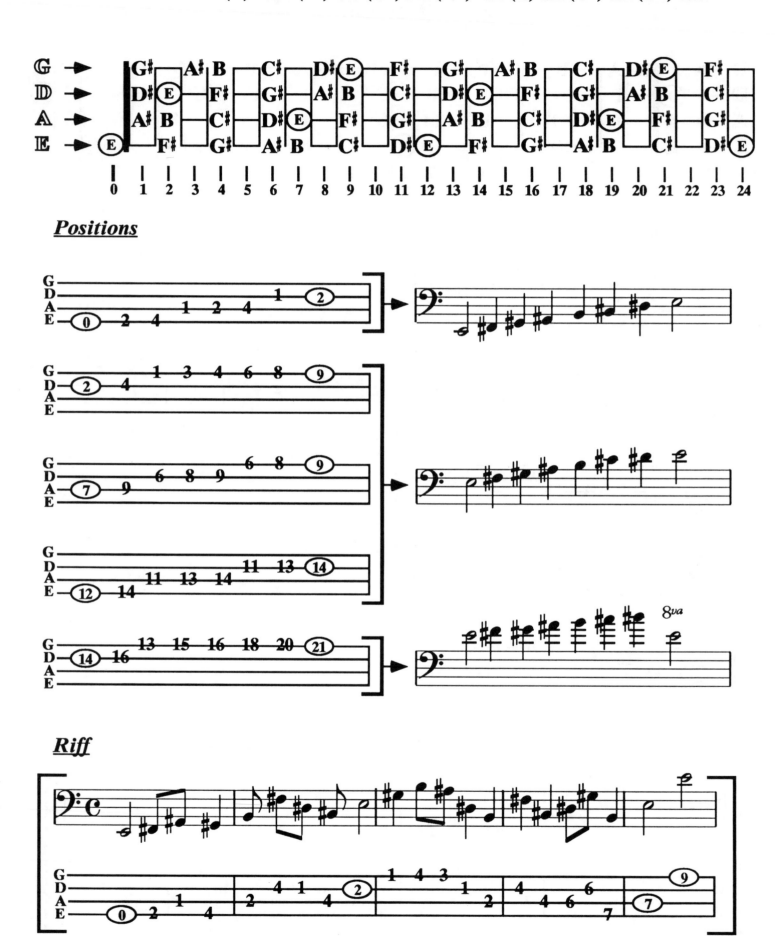

F LYDIAN MODE
FORMULA - (F) Root (G) 2nd (A) 3rd (B) ♮4th (C) 5th (D) 6th (E) 7th

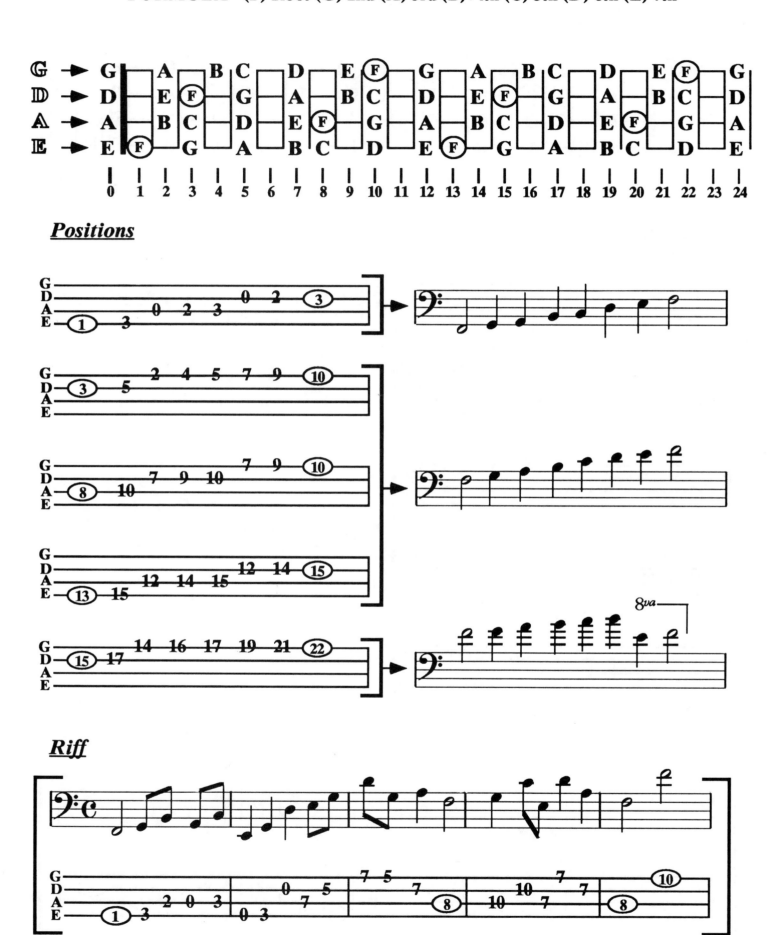

Positions

Riff

G LYDIAN MODE
FORMULA - (G) Root (A) 2nd (B) 3rd (C♯) ♯4th (D) 5th (E) 6th (F♯) 7th

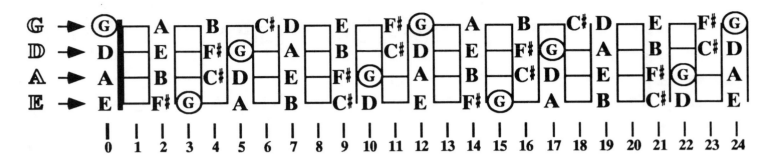

Positions

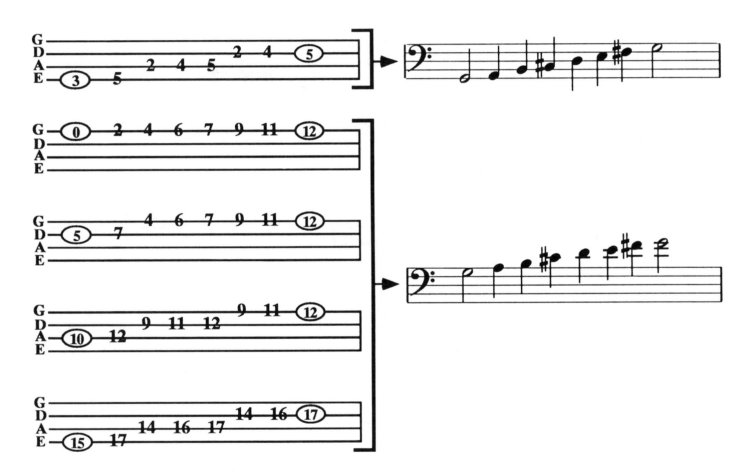

Riff

A LYDIAN MODE
FORMULA - (A) Root (B) 2nd (C#) 3rd (D#) #4th (E) 5th (F#) 6th (G#) 7th

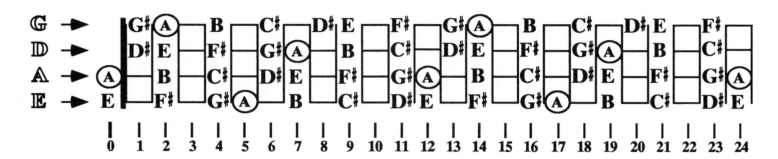

Positions

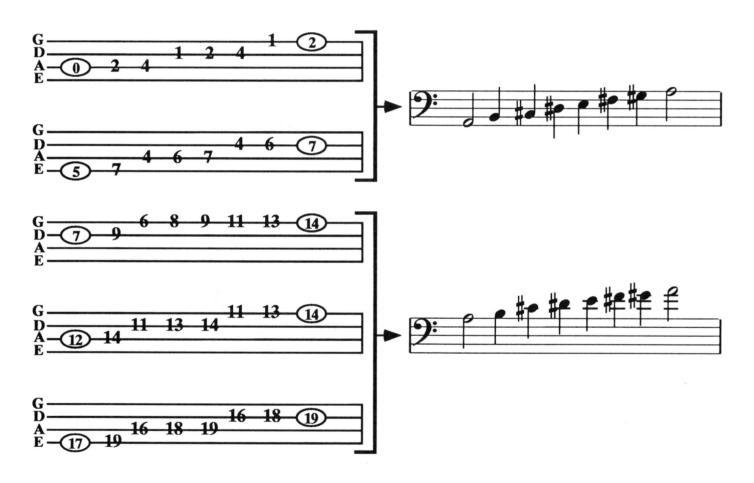

Riff

75

B LYDIAN MODE
FORMULA - (B) Root (C#) 2nd (D#) 3rd (E#) #4th (F#) 5th (G#) 6th (A#) 7th

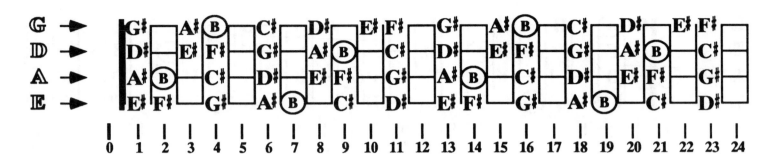

Positions

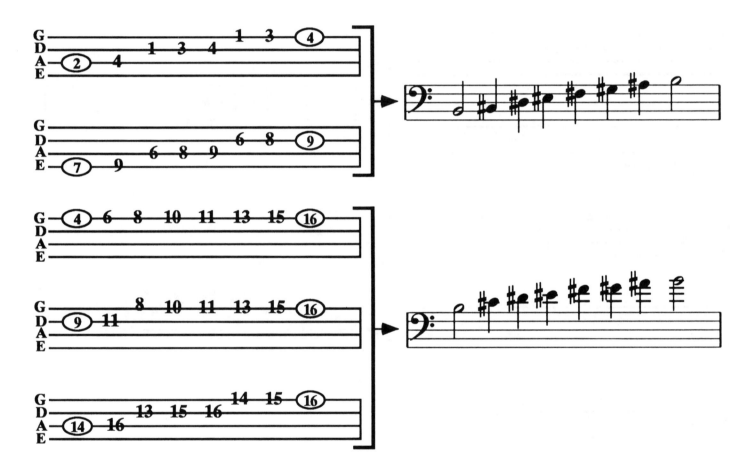

Riff

76

C PHRYGIAN MODE
FORMULA - (C) Root (D♭) ♭2nd (E♭) ♭3rd (F) 4th (G) 5th (A♭) ♭6th (B♭) ♭7th

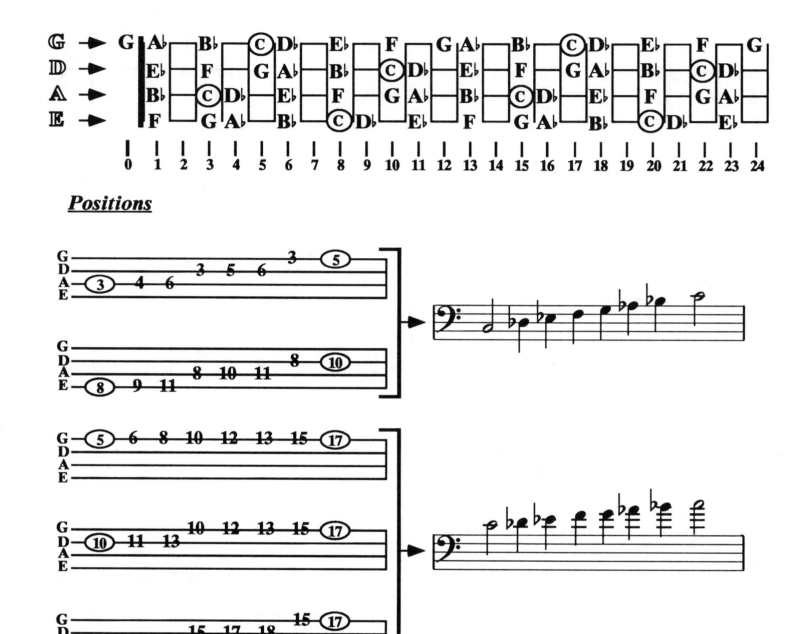

Positions

Riff

D PHRYGIAN MODE
FORMULA - (D) Root (E♭) ♭2nd (F) ♭3rd (G) 4th (A) 5th (B♭) ♭6th (C) ♭7th

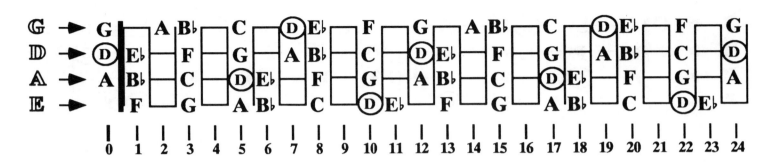

Positions

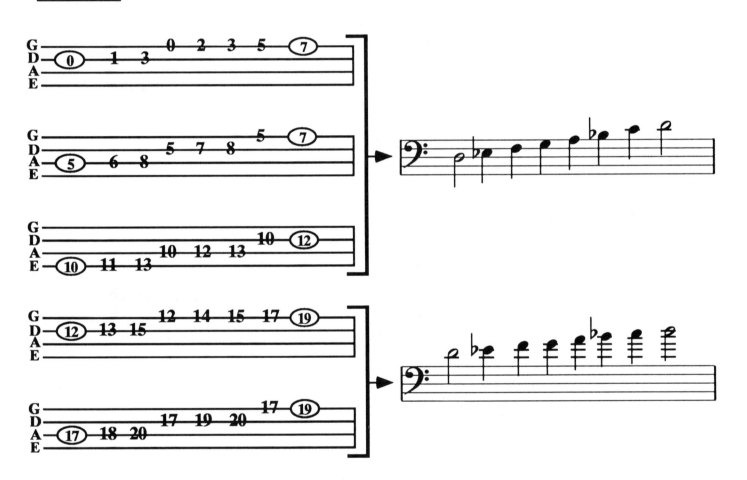

Riff

E PHRYGIAN MODE
FORMULA - (E) Root (F) ♭2nd (G) ♭3rd (A) 4th (B) 5th (C) ♭6th (D) ♭7th

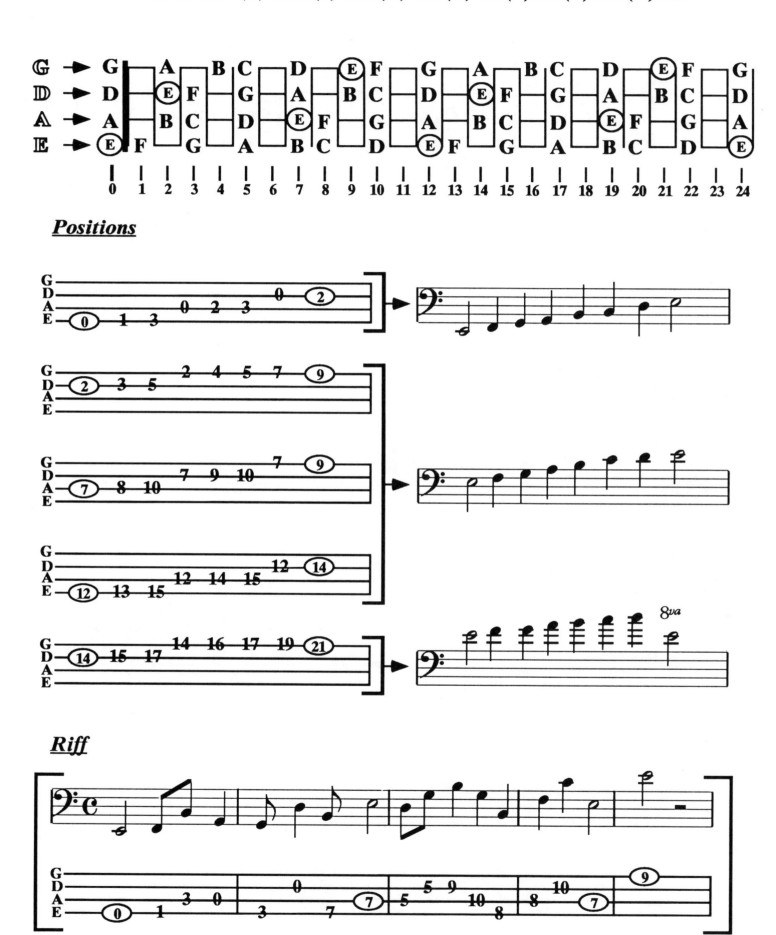

Positions

Riff

F PHRYGIAN MODE
FORMULA - (F) Root (G♭) ♭2nd (A♭) ♭3rd (B♭) 4th (C) 5th (D♭) ♭6th (E♭) ♭7th

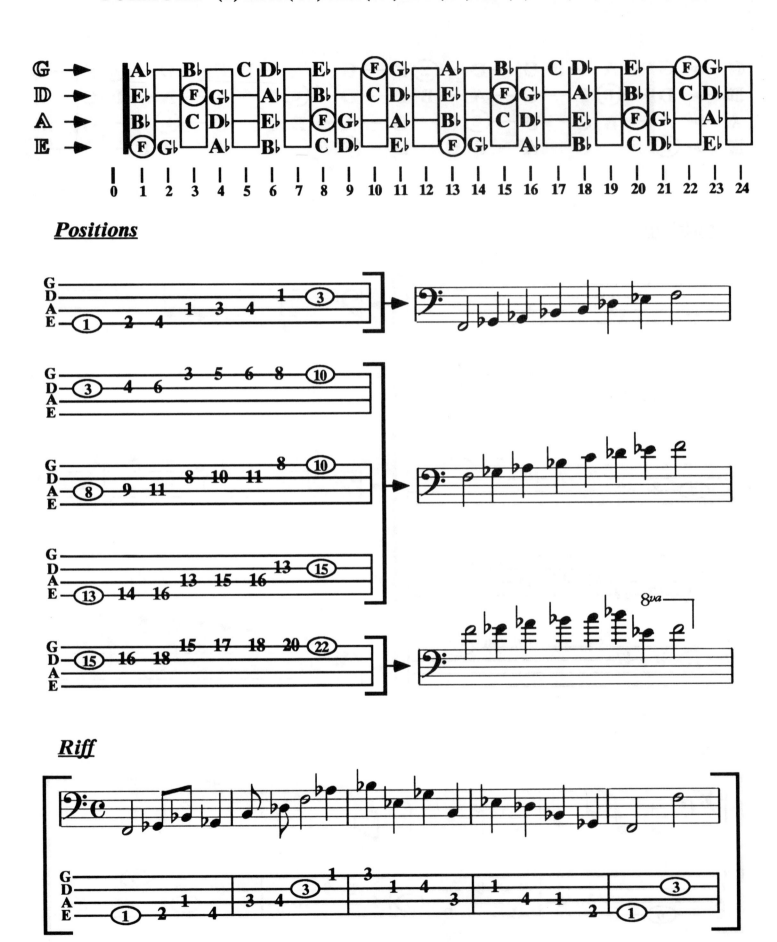

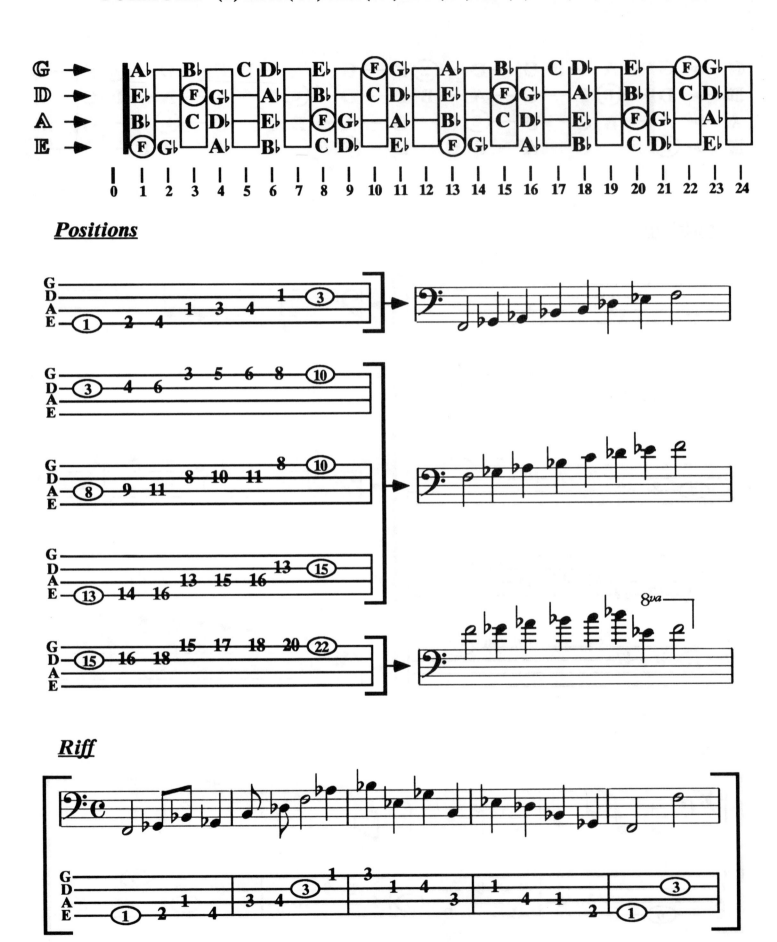

G PHRYGIAN MODE
FORMULA - (G) Root (A♭) ♭2nd (B♭) ♭3rd (C) 4th (D) 5th (E♭) ♭6th (F) ♭7th

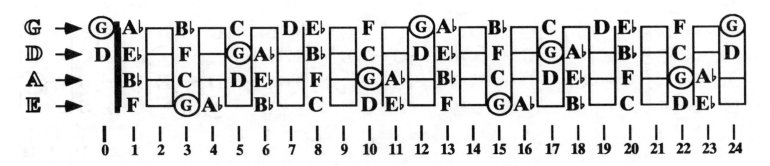

Positions

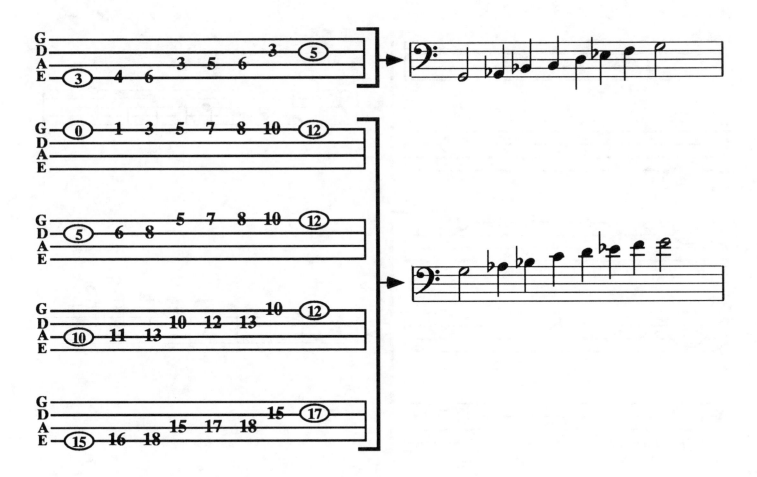

Riff

A PHRYGIAN MODE
FORMULA - (A) Root (B♭) ♭2nd (C) ♭3rd (D) 4th (E) 5th (F) ♭6th (G) ♭7th

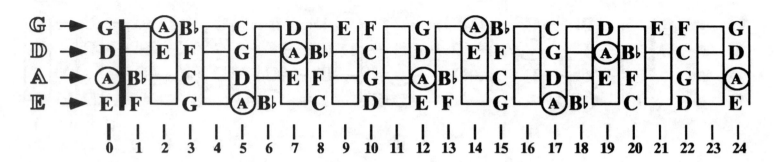

Positions

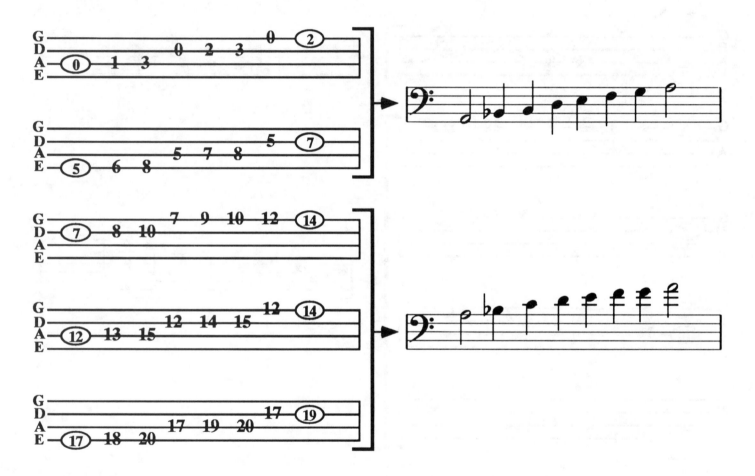

Riff

82

B PHRYGIAN MODE
FORMULA - (B) Root (C) ♭2nd (D) ♭3rd (E) 4th (F♯) 5th (G) ♭6th (A) ♭7th

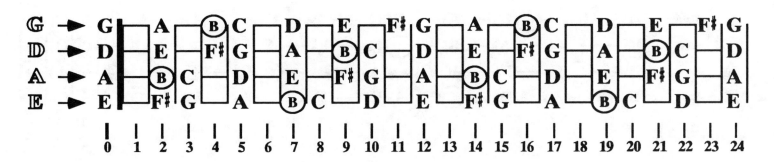

Positions

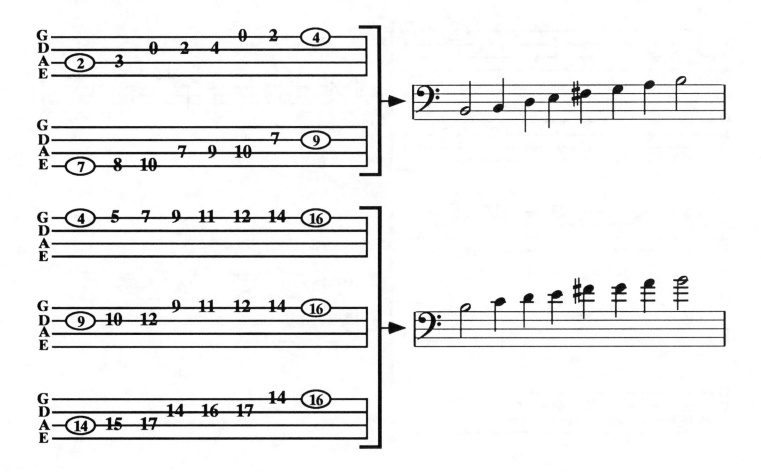

Riff

C LOCRIAN MODE
FORMULA - (C) Root (D♭) ♭2nd (E♭) ♭3rd (F) 4th (G♭) ♭5th (A♭) ♭6th (B♭) ♭7th

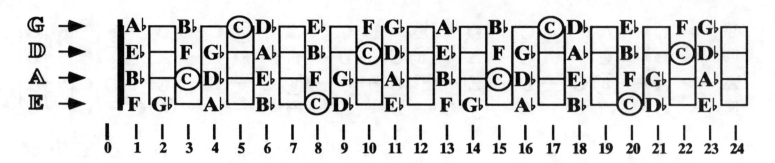

Positions

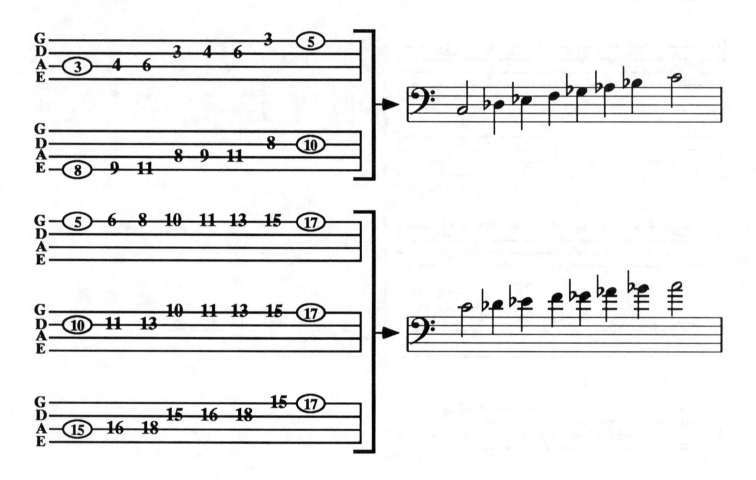

Riff

84

D LOCRIAN MODE
FORMULA - (D) Root (E♭) ♭2nd (F) ♭3rd (G) 4th (A♭) ♭5th (B♭) ♭6th (C) ♭7th

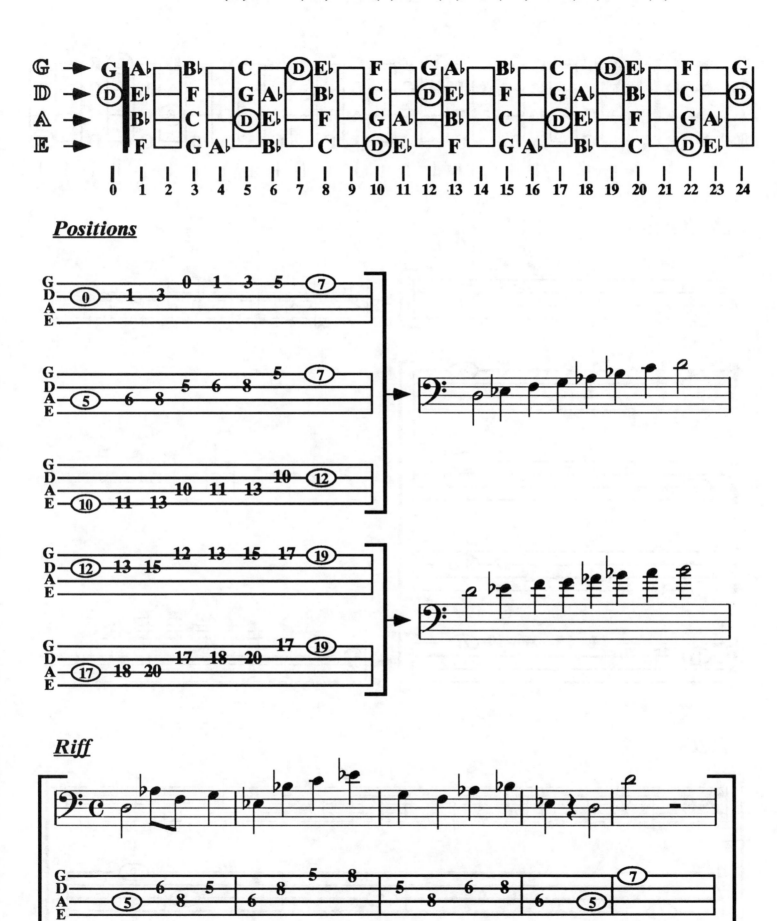

Positions

Riff

E LOCRIAN MODE
FORMULA - (E) Root (F) ♭2nd (G) ♭3rd (A) 4th (B♭) ♭5th (C) ♭6th (D) ♭7th

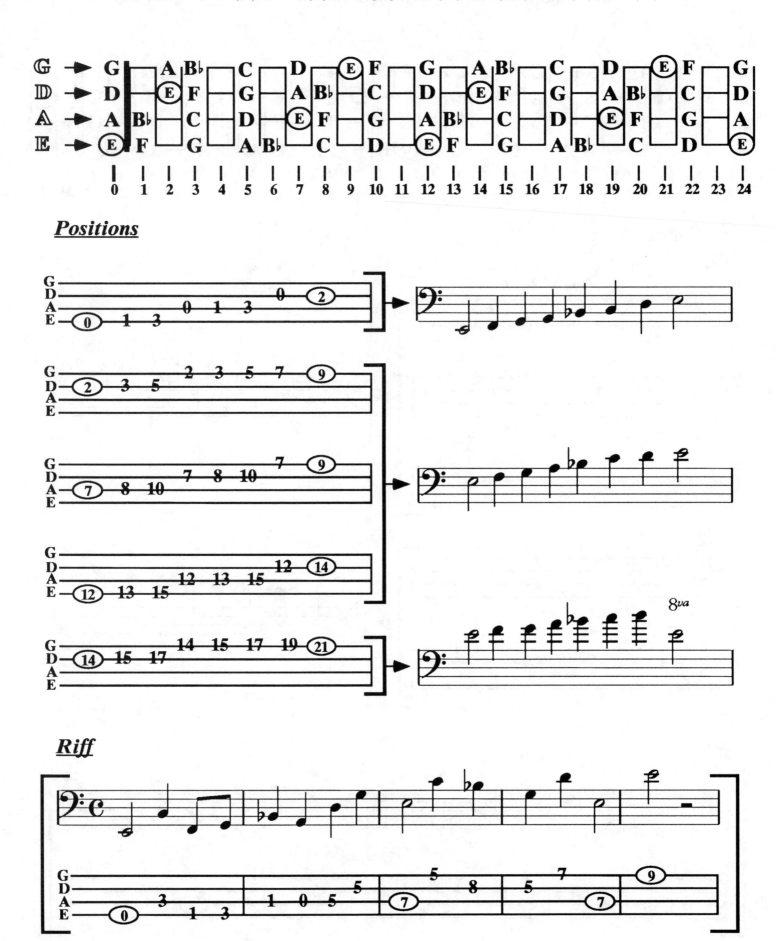

Positions

Riff

F LOCRIAN MODE
FORMULA - (F) Root (G♭) ♭2nd (A♭) ♭3rd (B♭) 4th (C♭) ♭5th (D♭) ♭6th (E♭) ♭7th

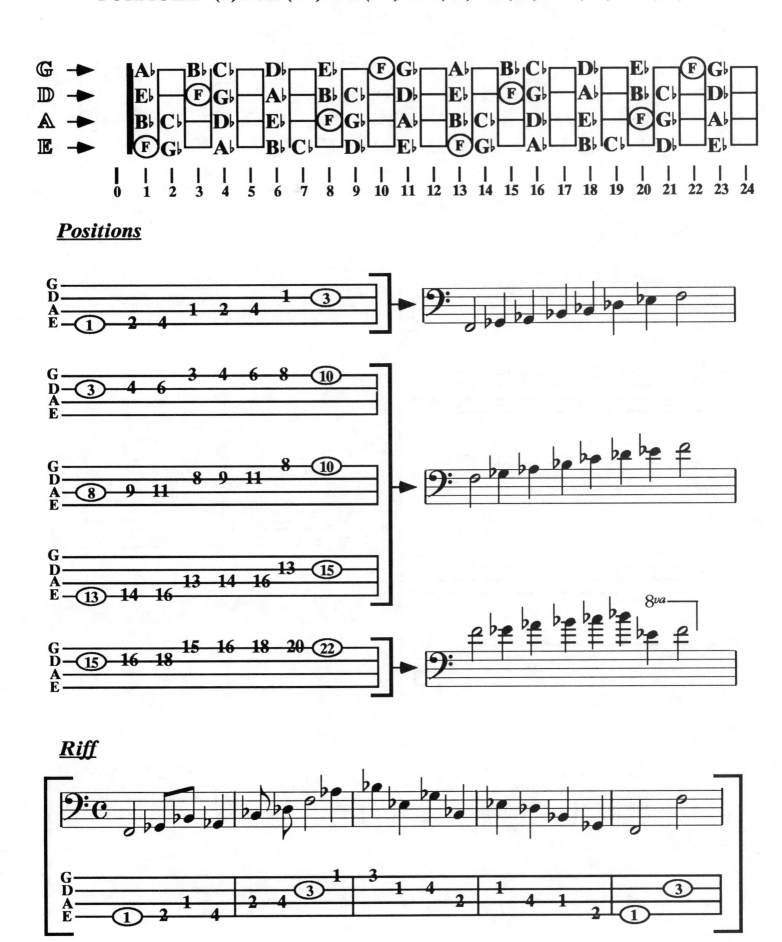

Positions

Riff

G LOCRIAN MODE
FORMULA - (G) Root (A♭) ♭2nd (B♭) ♭3rd (C) 4th (D♭) ♭5th (E♭) ♭6th (F) ♭7th

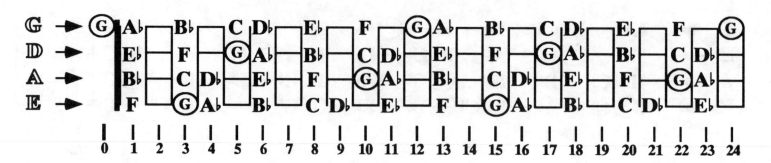

Positions

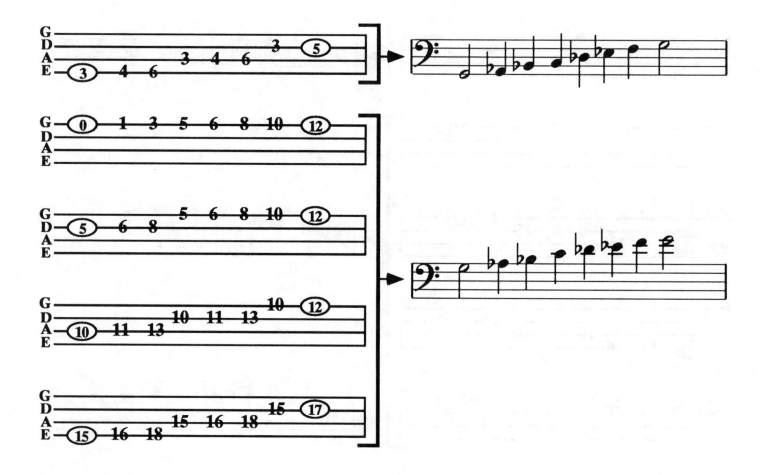

Riff

A LOCRIAN MODE
FORMULA - (A) Root (B♭) ♭2nd (C) ♭3rd (D) 4th (E♭) ♭5th (F) ♭6th (G) ♭7th

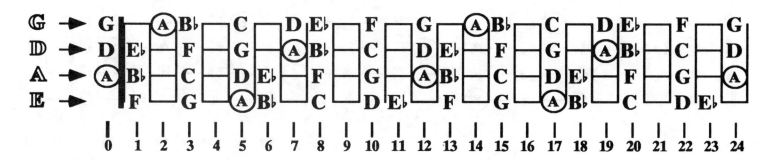

Positions

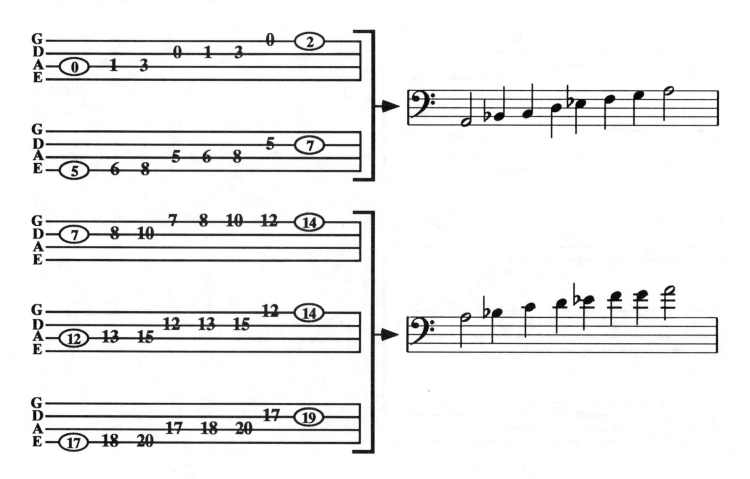

Riff

B LOCRIAN MODE
FORMULA - (B) Root (C) ♭2nd (D) ♭3rd (E) 4th (F) ♭5th (G) ♭6th (A) ♭7th

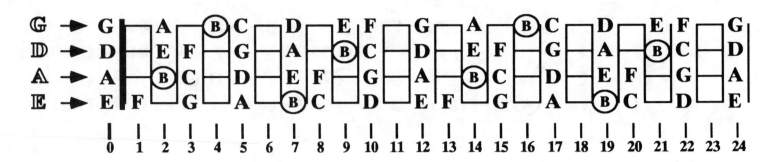

Positions

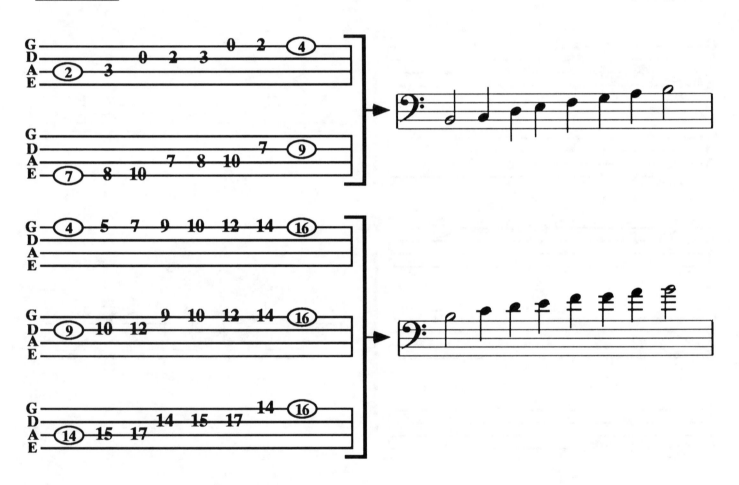

Riff

C HARMONIC MINOR
FORMULA - (C) Root (D) 2nd (E♭) ♭3rd (F) 4th (G) 5th (A♭) ♭6th (B) 7th

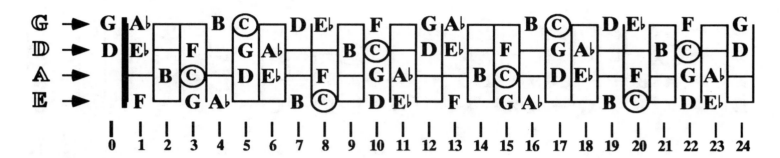

Positions

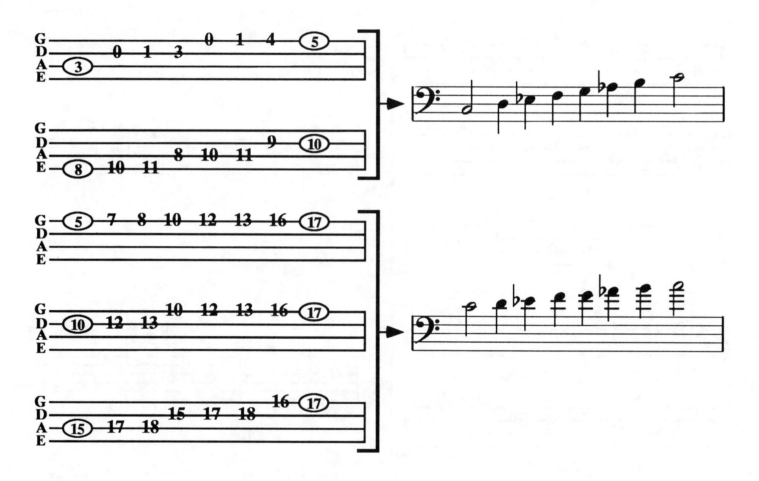

Riff

91

D HARMONIC MINOR
FORMULA - (D) Root (E) 2nd (F) ♭3rd (G) 4th (A) 5th (B♭)♭6th (C♯) 7th

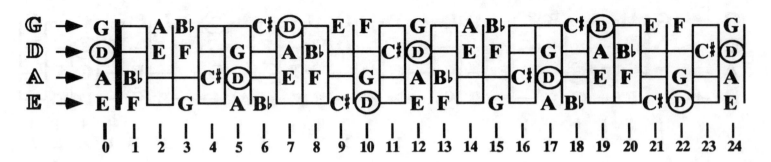

Positions

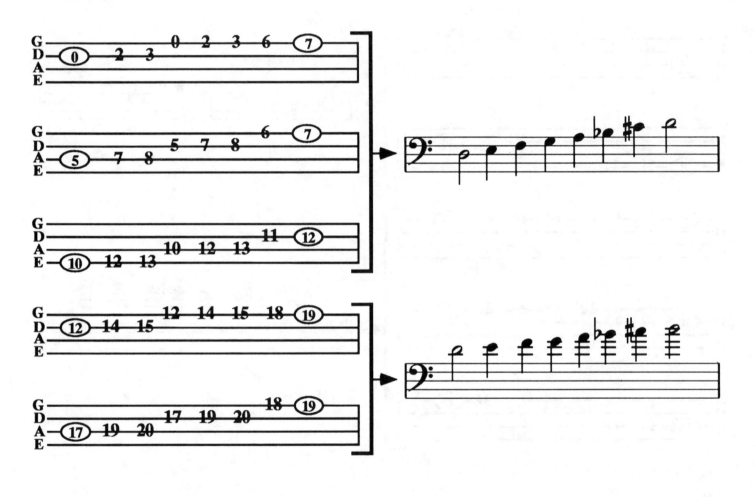

Riff

92

E HARMONIC MINOR
FORMULA - (E) Root (F♯) 2nd (G) ♭3rd (A) 4th (B) 5th (C) ♭6th (D♮) 7th

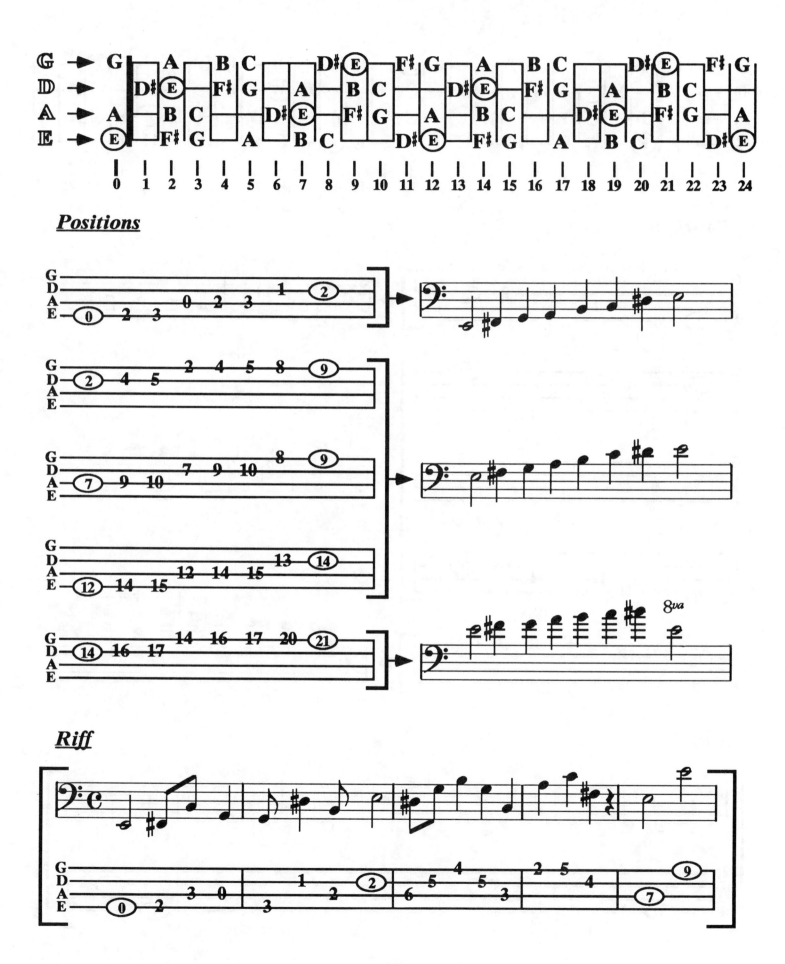

F HARMONIC MINOR
FORMULA - (F) Root (G) 2nd (A♭) ♭3rd (B♭) 4th (C) 5th (D♭) ♭6th (E) 7th

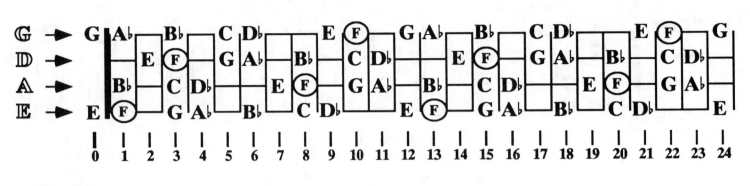

Positions

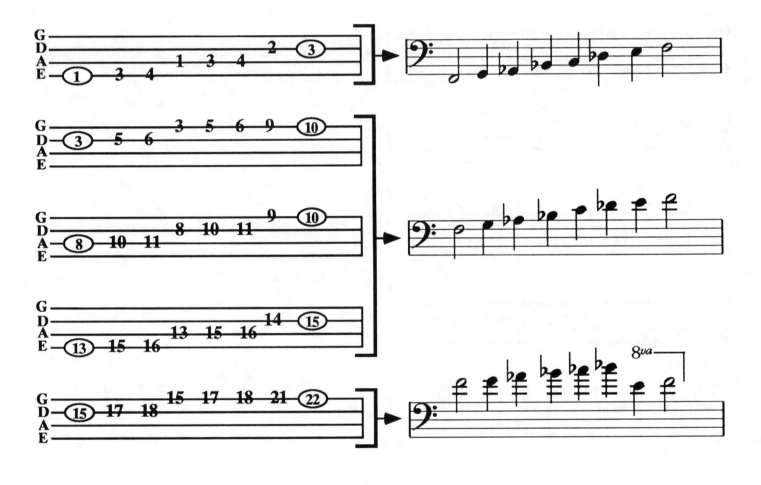

Riff

94

G HARMONIC MINOR
FORMULA - (G) Root (A) 2nd (B♭) ♭3rd (C) 4th (D) 5th (E♭) ♭6th (F#) 7th

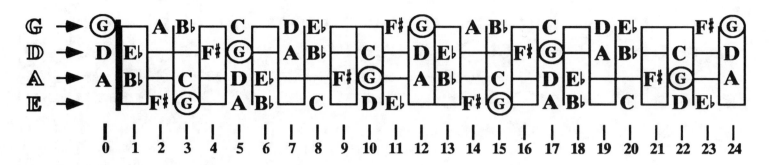

Positions

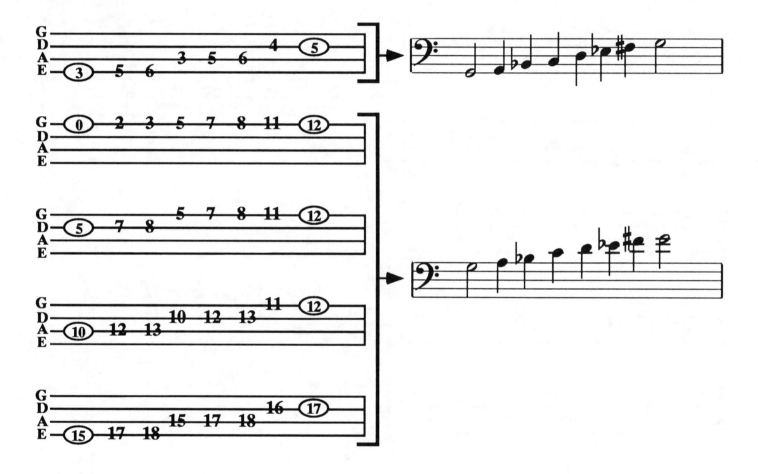

Riff

95

A HARMONIC MINOR
FORMULA - (A) Root (B) 2nd (C) ♭3rd (D) 4th (E) 5th (F) ♭6th (G♯) 7th

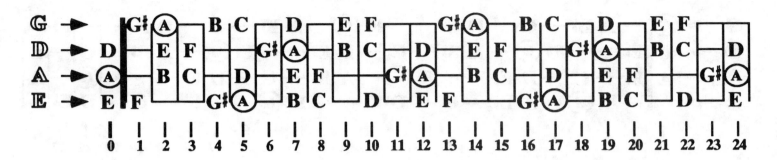

Positions

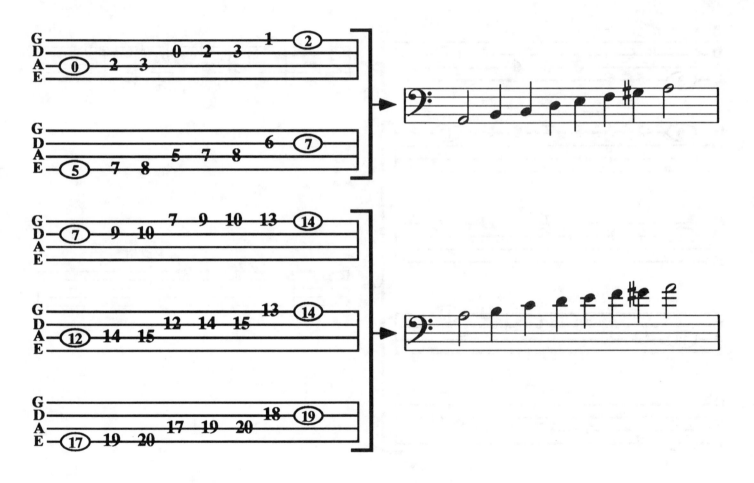

Riff

96

B HARMONIC MINOR
FORMULA - (B) Root (C♯) 2nd (D) ♭3rd (E) 4th (F♯) 5th (G) ♭6th (A♯) 7th

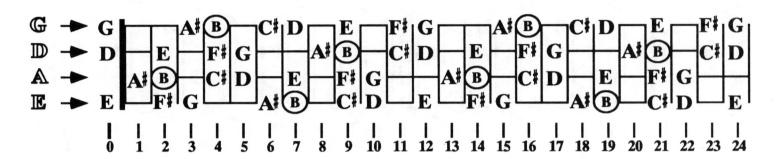

Positions

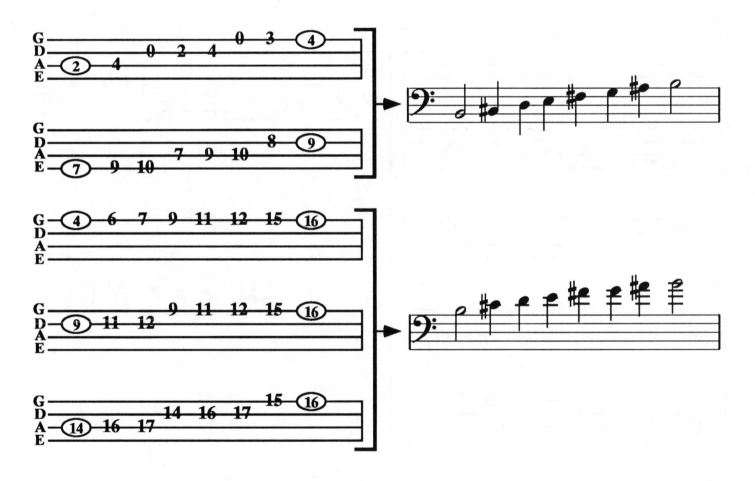

Riff

C MELODIC MINOR
FORMULA - (C) Root (D) 2nd (E♭) ♭3rd (F) 4th (G) 5th (A) 6th (B) 7th

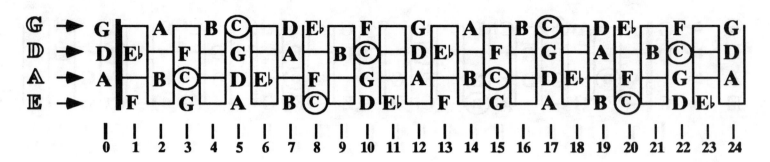

Positions

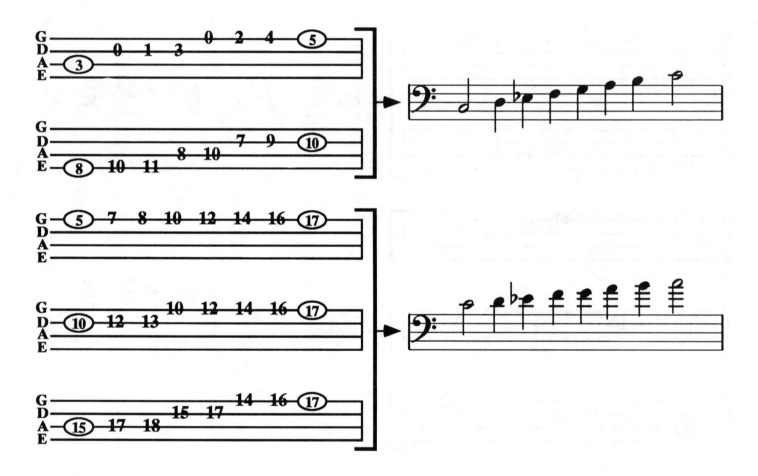

Riff

D MELODIC MINOR
FORMULA - (D) Root (E) 2nd (F) ♭3rd (G) 4th (A) 5th (B) 6th (C♯) 7th

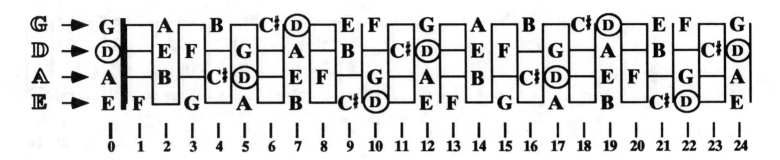

Positions

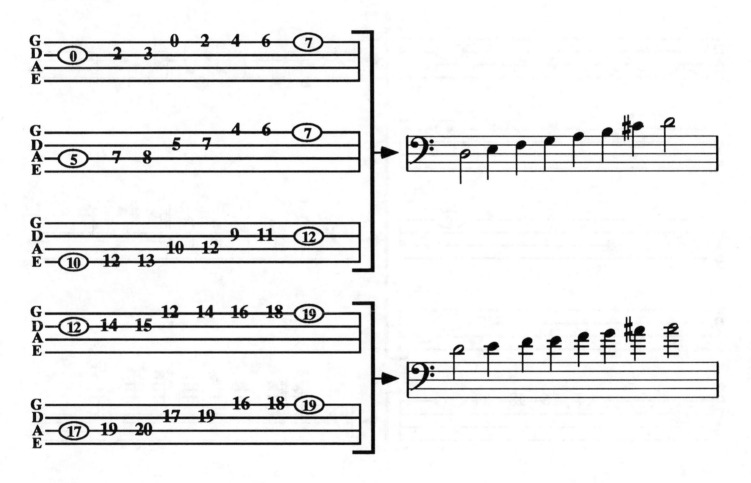

Riff

E MELODIC MINOR
FORMULA - (E) Root (F♯) 2nd (G) ♭3rd (A) 4th (B) 5th (C♯) 6th (D♯) 7th

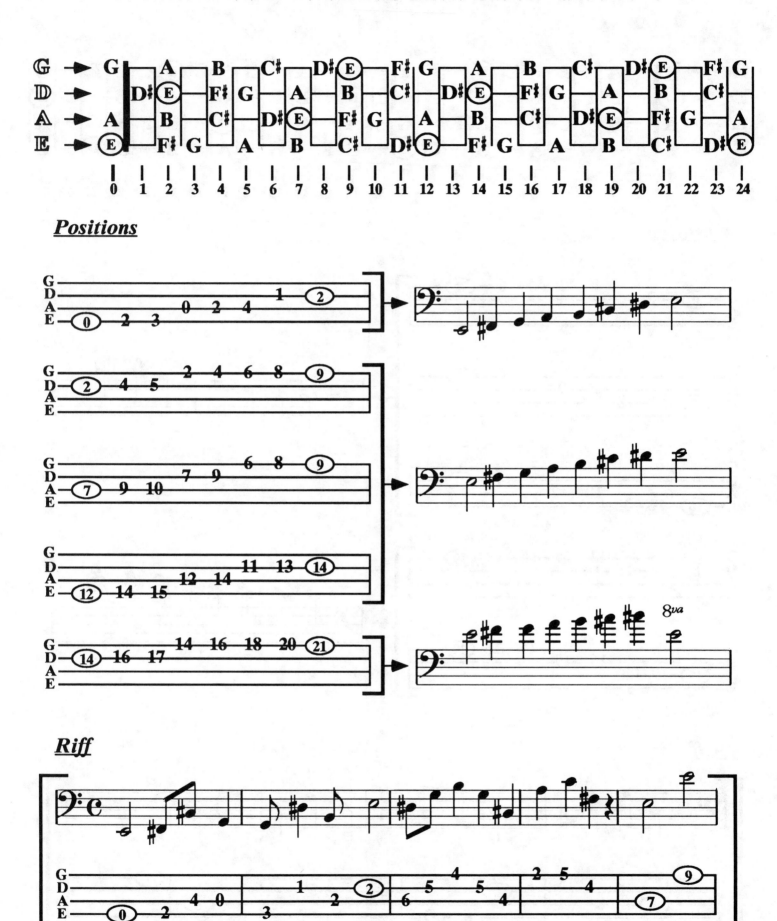

Positions

Riff

F MELODIC MINOR
FORMULA - (F) Root (G) 2nd (A♭) ♭3rd (B♭) 4th (C) 5th (D) 6th (E) 7th

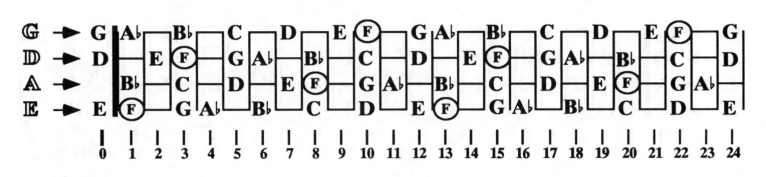

Positions

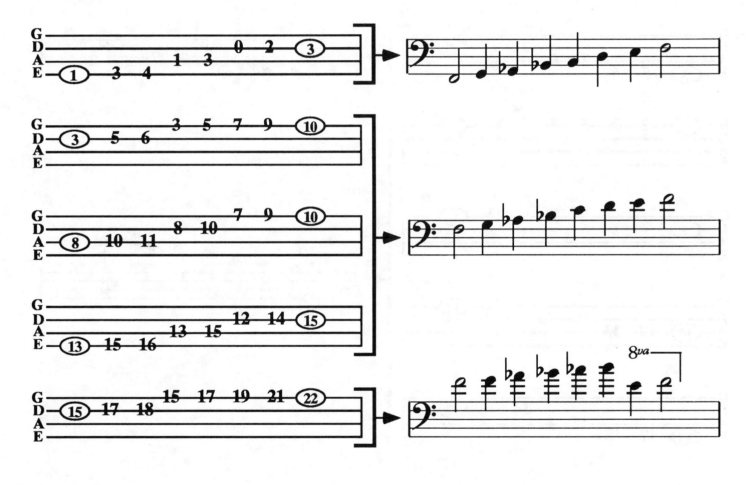

Riff

101

G MELODIC MINOR
FORMULA - (G) Root (A) 2nd (B♭) ♭3rd (C) 4th (D) 5th (E) 6th (F♯) 7th

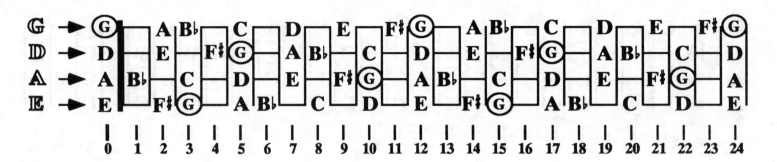

Positions

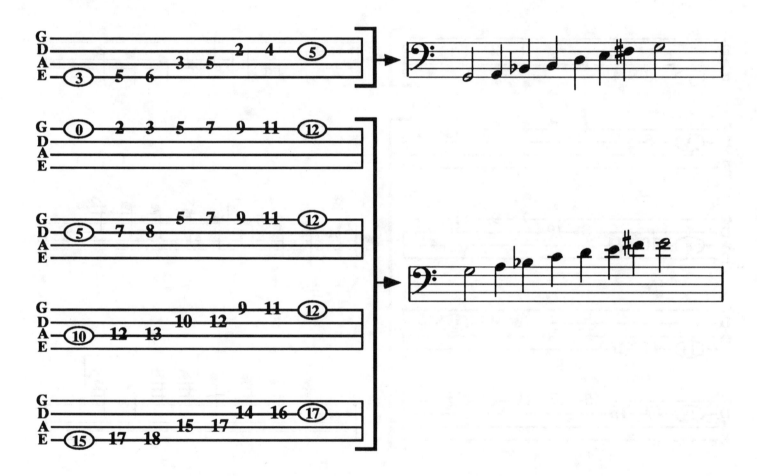

Riff

A MELODIC MINOR
FORMULA - (A) Root (B) 2nd (C) ♭3rd (D) 4th (E) 5th (F♮) 6th (G♮) 7th

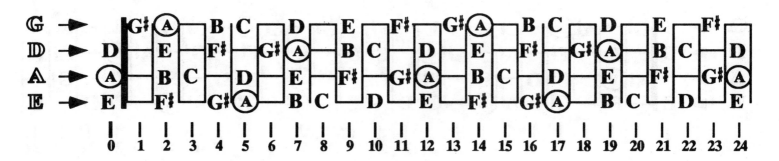

Positions

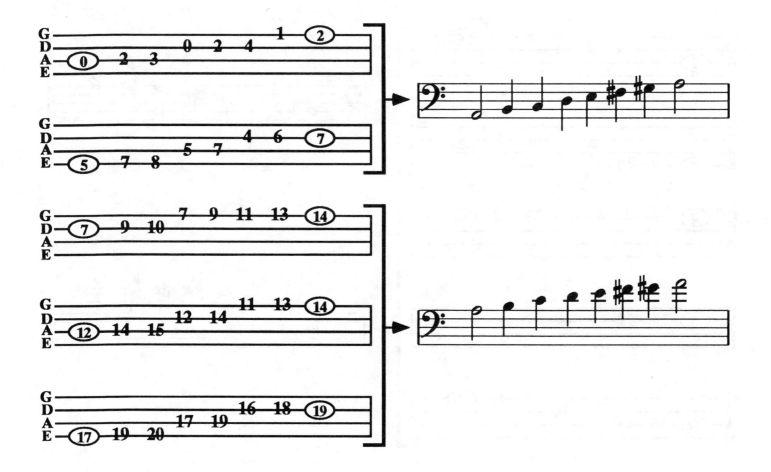

Riff

B MELODIC MINOR
FORMULA - (B) Root (C#) 2nd (D) ♭3rd (E) 4th (F#) 5th (G#) 6th (A#) 7th

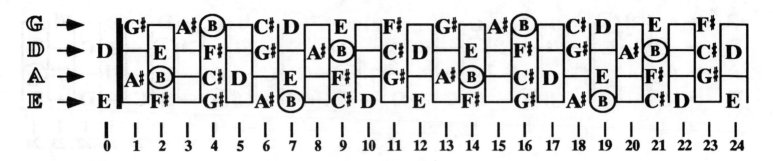

Positions

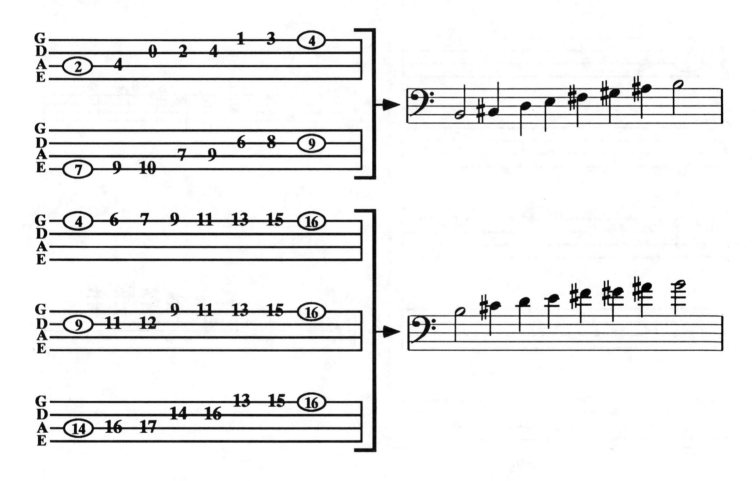

Riff